I KILLED A RAT

TRUE TALES FROM WILD PLACES

DAN BROOKLYN

An SOS Media creation
www.wearefr.ee

For you.
Who else?

CONTENTS

Hey, it's Dan.

Thanks for taking the time to read this. I know you've got other things going on, like jogging or drinking or making out with someone you love.

I've spent the last chunk of my adult life attempting to, among other things, live *in* the world. By that, I mean traveling to distant corners of the globe and trying to live a normal life.

Of course, what could have been considered normal several years ago has decayed into something different, but it happened gradually, and I never noticed.

Here are a few snippets that have shaped my life. I've tried to take out all the boring stuff and cut right to the good parts. I hope you like them, because that's really the point.

1. All events happened as described.
2. Some conversations have been downsized for readability
3. The math isn't always right, but it all adds up.

I'd love to hear what you think.

—DB

db@sosmedia.org
More stories on www.wearefr.ee

I

CULTURE

SNOW LION

Dharamsala, India

I was walking out of a day-long speech by The Dalai Lama feeling let down. Was I being punished for the hypocritical $5 Chinese radio I'd bought to listen to the live translation? The fucking thing was impossible to tune. Instead of the Dalai Lama, I mostly heard brain-melt static and Russian at irregular volumes. My eardrums hurt.

To summarize, The Dalai Lama's messages were:

1. Does God exist? Buddhism doesn't give a shit.
2. Don't hate. Meditate.

The thousand Dalai Lama groupies poured hungrily into the honking, cramped streets of Dharamsala. Lunch time. At the corner of a busy intersection, clearly the coolest Tibetan dude in the city approached me with a flyer. He had bug-eye shades covering half his face, big purple headphones around his neck, fire-red jeans, and a striped Adidas warm-up jacket.

— SNOW LION DANCE LIVE SHOW —

— AN UNFORGETTABLE EXPERIENCE —

He said, *Hello, please come tonight.*

I shook his hand in the coolest way I could and promised that I would.

I hid out in the hotel for a few hours, playing the most worthless game — seeing if I could count higher than "1" between the sound of honking traffic. I lost. I headed to the show.

He was still standing there, we shook hands in a cool way again.

Hello! Good you come! Go down steps into school. I coming soon, thank you, ok!

I gave him 250 Rupees ($4) and pretended to ignore the other 7 tourists milling around the school who were pretending to ignore me while we waited for the Snow Lion, if that was his real name, to come down.

A swarm of little school kids more or less pushed us into one of the concrete classrooms. We sat on foam pads in a few neat rows. The walls were hand-painted with flowers, mountains and huge raindrops. A Tibetan flag hung next to a framed, smiling photo of the Dalai Lama.

Welcome, everyone. He bowed formally. *This is traditional Tibet dance.*

He wrestled a vest and a skirt from a duffel bag, pulled them on over his clothes, lit a tall white candle, and fiddled with some buttons until thin, overly-loud music blared from his boombox.

He did a slow, deliberate, seemingly culturally-appropriate dance involving turning half way, bending slightly, turning the other way and bending slightly. If it wasn't so bizarre, it would have been boring as hell.

He snapped off the music after it seemed we had all gotten the point.

Thank you. Next dance not traditional Tibet dance. Please be happy. Thank you.

He clicked on the next track and started spinning. The music was quivering, high-pitched, Indian-sounding. There's a way that dancers spin where they whip around in a controlled way, keeping their eyes mostly focused on one spot so they don't get dizzy. He did not do that. He held his head in his hands like someone having bad thoughts and he spun the way you or I might do it, unprofessionally running in little circles, trying not to fall over. He was like a spinning top, catching tiny cracks in the sidewalk and jumping around.

But he did not fall over.

His wild, curly black hair became matted with sweat. The kids in the back of the class giggled. The eight spectators glanced at each other, finally, to confirm that he had been spinning for an absurdly long time. Ten, twelve, fifteen minutes? Who can measure time?

He spun so long that I forgot where I was.

He tore off the vest, then his shirt. A long belt of red fabric appeared from somewhere and he began rudely tying it around his face, tighter and tighter, until his cheeks were red and his eyes were blindfolded. He was spinning more violently, getting closer to the wall. I frowned. The German woman covered her mouth. He slammed into the wall. The kids in the back laughed, so the rest of us let out our held breath. He rebounded, and, now knowing where the wall was, he spun faster and faster, then lunged at the wall, banging harshly into the solid concrete. Again and again. Sweat sprang from his body. His skull hit the wall with a cracking sound. He left impressions of himself on the wall.

I took a few seconds of video to prove this was happening, and on the video I laugh nervously and say Jesus.

Then, he casually slipped off the blindfold.

Thank you. Everyone please. Be happy and be free. Everything will be alright. Thank you.

He clicked through to the next track; unearthly deep sounds of chanting monks. He knelt on the floor and put his hands in prayer, then crawled towards the Asian couple next to me. He grabbed her face by the sides and stared deeply into her eyes. He lunged forward and pressed his forehead forcefully onto hers. Their third eyes were touching. He stared into her eyes unflinchingly. She smiled for a second, then her cheeks sank and became deadly serious. The kids in the back whispered, laughed, and went silent. He held her for an uncomfortably long time before he released her, did a short bow with his head and dove at me. He grabbed the back of my head so I couldn't look away. His hair dripped sweat onto my face and shirt. His eyes were wild and circular inside his sharp Tibetan features. His forehead pressed heavy, sweaty.

I stopped being a tourist, then.

This is what it's like, Dan. This is what it's like to be me. To be a refugee. To be Tibetan. To have your home taken. To be lost.

LOOK AT ME.

I understood that his dance was a communication. He could use words and say that China destroyed multitudes of temples, and we might imagine it somehow and then feel the result of our own thoughts, but it's not real. We're just feeling our own assumption of feelings. But that face. Staring into that hungry, painful face until thoughts dissolve — is an understanding beyond language.

Sorry. I skipped ahead. I forgot the part where he told us about how he left Tibet with his family and snuck into India. How the border police jailed them and how they spent months suffering from dysentery and near-starvation in a wretched Indian prison. What it was like to helplessly, angrily watch his mother nearly die of weakness and dehydration — for freedom from the Chinese regime.

We nodded because we were from the United States, Canada, Germany and Japan, and we were good people who didn't approve of stomping out cultures — we came here to see the Dalai Lama — we believe in human rights.

But as he crawled from one of us to the other, sweating, staring, breathing on us — he had to tackle the German woman — he straddled her and pinned her head down to the cold concrete floor with his forehead and we watched her mouth tighten to keep from drinking his sweat.

There's no escape.

THIS IS WHAT IT'S LIKE his eyes screamed in a language that we all understand. The language of pain. The language of the human spirit's desire to be free.

After he made his round through all eight of us, he bowed politely.

Thank you. This is my dance. When I dance, I am happy. Wish you all good friendship and health for you family and happy life.

He turned and snapped off the chanting monks, sat on the floor and collected himself. I crawled over to him.

I said, "Thank you. That was the best... dance... I've ever seen."

He smiled and held out his hand. I opened my arms and I hugged him. He was totally sweaty and gross and I pretended not to care. I wanted to let him know that I was not afraid of him, not afraid to look at his pain, that I understood the plight of his people.

My eyes said, "I know what it's like."

And his said, *nice try.*

SPEECHES

Cape Town, South Africa

Tap tap

I'm too drunk to do a speech, I thought as I tested the microphone with my finger.

"Hi everybody."

Somebody shouted: DAAAAAN! *Wooooot!*

I'd been warned: Do it early. Don't wait until you're drunk and everyone else is drunk. Make it short.

Ok, I had said. Short and early and not drunk. It was none of these things.

Somebody who knew me shouted: WHO ARE YOU???

"I'm the best man, bitch."

In my mind, there was laughter.

I dove in. "What makes David different is his heart. His love for his friends. Dave, Moni, who we are, standing around you, are people who couldn't be anywhere else. You're standing—well, sitting— with people who believe in you. Thank you for bringing us here, for gathering us from the far corners of the globe. We love you guys."

Did I say bitch?

"Cheers."

I raised half-full glass of white wine. Alas, it was summer.

But that's not the interesting part. Fancy hotel atrium. International crowd. Button-downs, sunglasses, tinkling glassware, all good things.

I was slated to give another speech the next day, during the wedding dinner. I'd emailed reception so they could print it for me. I was on a roll.

They say black differently in South Africa. I don't know how to explain it, but in South Africa, it sounds different. Like it's the ultimate characteristic. The receptionist was black, but he was also probably in his early forties, had a circular, friendly face, and a chilled out, almost-whisper-voice. His name tag said Henry.

Henry was on the phone, head tilted.

Henry: I'm sorry, sir. I don't see your email.

DB: Henry, my man. Who you talking to? Your girl?

Henry: Not my girl, sir. Here, say hello.

Henry handed me the black hotel phone.

DB: Hello?

Phone: Hey… you Henry's friend?

DB: Sure. Henry and I are chillin.

Phone: Hey… ummmmm… you guys just chillin, na?

DB: Yea, chillin here at reception. I'm here for a wedding. Not my wedding though.

Phone: Oh… that's too bad.

DB: Why? Phone: You busy, neh?

DB: Where are you?

Phone: In my bed, baby. Just feelin… lazy. You voice soundin' so good.

DB: Baby? Jesus! You're sounding so sexy! I looked at Henry, who was biting his finger with his white teeth to stifle a laugh. I gave him WTF eyebrow raise, and he replied with IDK eyebrow raise with head shake. This endearing fake innocence.

Phone: You want to come find me, baby?

DB: Baby? What's your deal?

Phone: I ain't got no deal. Just feelin' this, that's all. Feelin' you. Nnnnnnn…

DB: I gotta get back. I'm the best man in this wedding, I have to drink with the people —

Phone: Awwww what? You don't gotta go.

DB: God! You sound — bah! Oh my God. How do I find you?

Phone: Get my number from Henry. Call me when you're done with your party, baby.

DB: Ok, baby. Stay hot.

Phone: Mmmmm… go. Hurry up. I handed the phone back to Henry.

DB: Henry! Who the fuck was that?

Henry: A friend of mine, sir.

DB: You know what she was saying to me?

Henry: She is very beautiful, sir. You would enjoy to call her, sir. He smiled. I don't know what that smile meant, exactly.

He handed me the paper copies of my speech and a classy, Winchester Mansion notecard with her phone number like a cherry on top.

For the next few hours, I repeated this story in increasingly drunker and therefore more vivid detail, until no one, including myself believed me.

Mars

MARS BAR

As spoken by Rene, an Estonian man, on a train through Laos

Mars Bar is for me the taste of freedom.
When I was kid,
Finally the iron curtain fell,
And my friend brings these Mars bars from Finland,
And I remember standing there on the side of the street,
Looking up at the sky
And biting into this candy bar
And I couldn't believe that
anything
in the
fucking world
could taste this good.
I chewed and I chewed
three Mars bars.
Then I threw up.
But now when I see this Mars bar,
I still remember this moment.
And for me,
this is the taste of freedom.

Do you want a bite?

No, that thing you got there looks all half eaten and melted. It looks like shit.

But it will taste like freedom.

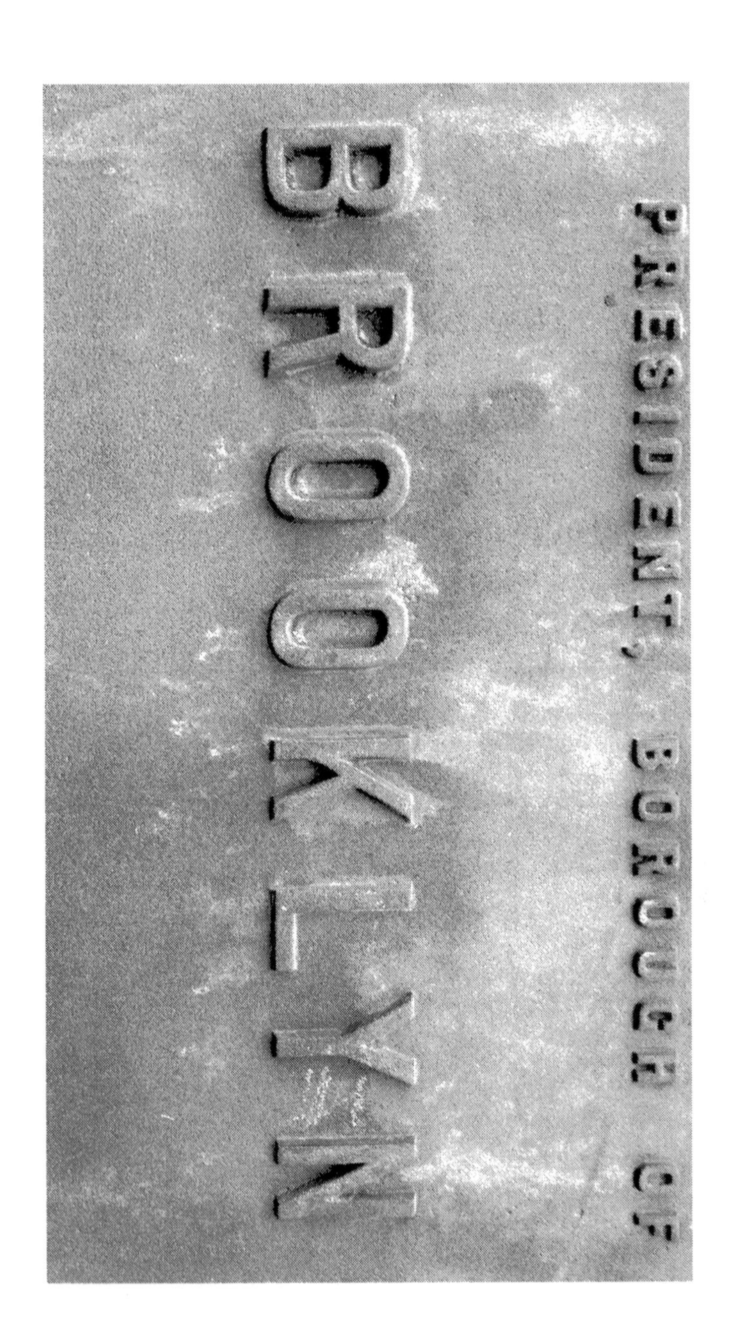
PRESIDENT, BOROUGH OF
BROOKLYN

WORDS IN NEW YORK

Bedford–Stuyvesant, Brooklyn, New York

R train
Flatbush
Verrazano Bridge
The Village
Battery Park
Bowery
The Frick
The Whitney

The city,
they say,
will chew you up and shit you out.
It's true.
Multiple New Yorker assholes said that to me.

I find the city much more bearable with headphones.
Then it's a gruesome Tool video, all these sideways mouths,

flat hats and misery.

I know it's my misery I see reflected I'm not stupid.

Battery Park
Coney Island

Everything sounds better in New York, too bad we're
so unhappy.

MEMORIAL DAY

Miraflores, Lima, Peru

G: What is Memorial Day celebrating?

DB: Oh, right, today is Memorial Day.

G: Well, for The States.

DB: Memorial Day remembers all the American… well, North American soldiers who died in combat.

G: I didn't know that North American soldiers could die.

DB: Very funny.

G: In the movies, American soldiers never die.

DB: There were a few back in World War Two.

G: They just keep getting more and more bloody.

DB: The wars or the people? Or the movies?

G: All of it. You don't seem very sad.

DB: I am, I'm sad.

G: You're not.

DB: Aren't you hungry or something? Can we go eat?

G: That's why you travel isn't it? Because you don't like your country.

DB: That's not true at all. I love my country.

G: Yes, all Americans say that. Like you're trained to say that.

DB: You think we're brainwashed or something?

G: You all have this cheesy love for your country. Like big cheesy smiles.

DB: You watch too much TV.

G: Still you guys are all like "I'm proud to be USA" and all that.

DB: Are you proud to be Peruvian?

G: Of course!

DB: See? Same cheesy smile.

G: You don't understand.

DB: I don't need to understand, I'm American.

G: You're such a dick. I'm American, too.

DB: Come on, let's go eat.

G: Yea, let's go get a hamburger for you.

DB: I'm vegetarian.

G: Then we will just drink beer today.

DB: OK. Deal. Jesus.

G: You want to bring Jesus into this now?

DB: No, no. Jesus. You're right.

FEAST OF MORALITY

Sun Moon Koon Village, Laos

V's village is best accessed by hiking through a bit of jungle and boating down the Nam Nga River. His family spends most of the year farming rice for food. The other months, his father sells his own hand-poured concrete beams to a local construction company.

Like many Laotians, V has very little access to money. V owns fewer changes of clothes than the average weekend traveller has folded in their valise. Paypal won't transfer money to Lao bank accounts, I've tried.

When I met V five years ago, he was a novice monk in Luang Prabang. In passing, he mentioned what he felt was the exorbitant cost of college: $250 per year. Yet he desperately wanted the opportunity to study and move himself out of poverty. I slipped him the cash on my way out of town.

We kept in touch through email and then Facebook. He was always sending blessings and good wishes and thanks.

Four years later, he walked with a degree in civil law. Then he headed back to his village to help his family with the rice harvest.

When I arrived at this table at this particular moment in V's life, a law job near his village had opened up. Two job openings. Over a hundred applicants were lined up to take the entrance exam.

The year prior, V's friend had gotten the same job at the same government firm. His advice: "It doesn't matter how well you do on the test. If you want the job, pay four million kip."

That's around five hundred US dollars; a spendy sum for most anyone. A meager bribe by some standards.

I thought about it for the days we spent together in his village. Was it possible to work around this speedbump of corruption?

On one hand, V could study and ace the exam and (maybe) they'd have to hire him. Could hard work and honesty win? He's already studying his law books through the nights. The risk: these job openings only open annually. Veracity could set V's career and monetary prospects back an entire year.

I tried planting seeds against corruption in his mind. V and I communicate well, except for this point. He doesn't seem to understand me when I speak about how corruption is the root of the impoverishment and misdistribution of wealth in the world today. Especially in developing nations like Laos. I tried making bold statements.

V, corruption is why your village doesn't have a school.

V, corruption is why we're riding in the back of a pickup truck and not on public transportation.

V, corruption is the reason your family is poor while other people drive around in fancy cars.

But V won't hear it right now. He's 24 and he wants a motorbike, an apartment, and a girlfriend. He wants money. If corruption brings those things, then he wants corruption, too.

On my last night, V's family sat with me on the sparsely furnished floor of his cousin's house. Baskets of sticky rice between us. Small bowls of searing hot, lime-flavored dip. Duck curry. Pig's blood soup. A feast. Afterwards, we sat back on a long, hand-hewn table and sipped BeerLao. I offered him the four million, but asked that he pay back half within a year. He agreed.

Research into the effectivity of NGOs and charities concluded: just give them money. Don't try to dig their wells, plant their seeds, pave their streets or build their schools. Just give money to people who need it and let them sort it out.

You can give a man a fish and he'll eat for a day... but you can give a man four million kip and let him live his life the way that it makes sense to him.

This week I received a text from V. He paid the bribe. Five million, actually; an additional million from his parents.

He got the job.

I fear that once he is motorbiking the streets of Luang Prabang, girlfriend's arms around his waist, he might conclude that maybe this corruption thing isn't so bad.

His family sold their garden to afford a year's rent for an apartment near his new office: $420 US dollars. His job as a civil lawyer starts in May.

V messaged me: `I want be corrupt lawyer so I have money visit you America :)`

A joke?

GATORS

Machu Picchu, Peru

YOU'RE A *GATOR! I'M* A GATOR!
WHAT'R THE *CHANCES!?*

She spoke in all caps. I pitied her husband; I pitied my friend.

You know that photo of Machu Picchu — the one where your friend looks like a postcard adventurer, posed above the Peruvian Andes? Well, when you get there, assume you'll need to wait behind about six hundred other people who have taken tour busses to that exact spot.

We'd only made it a few yards from the stream of buses. The Japanese followed a Japanese guide with a Japanese flag hoisted high on a stick. The Russians, the Italians, the French.

Dy's shirt said Steamers Restaurant, Gainesville, Florida.

MY SISTER JANET'S A GATOR! JANET! *JAAAAAA*NET!
WE GOT A *GATOR* HERE!

Her voice echoed down into the stone walls of the ancient city.

Y'ALL SHOULD JUMP ON OUR TOUR!

Dy hit my chest. Sometimes the loudest screams are whispers. He mouthed: *Run.*

We turned and ran. Away from Machu Picchu, from the ancient, perfect ruins floating in Andean clouds, away from these flags.

The ancient trail that the Incans used still whirls through the Andes like a roller coaster. We sprinted up and down into the crystal, thin air.

A vision of cresting these berms in the morning light, having walked for days — seeing this temple high in the Andes. A thousand years ago, they'd have nothing to compare anything to. Just beauty the way beauty should be, incomparable.

We looked back at the floating thumbnail of ruins.

Dy: I'm blocking this out.

DB: Yes, let's not remember this.

Dy: Fat Americans.

DB: She was so happy to see you.

Dy: Who does a tour of anything anymore?

DB: People who like facts.

Dy: People who like to be lied to.

DB: Isn't that everyone?

Dy: Not me.

He was right. Dylan fuels his mind with science. If he finds you liking Paulo Cohelo, he'll send you a 15 page study called *On the Reception and Detection of Pseudo-Profound Bullshit.* You can't persuade him with emotions or adjectives — only facts. He broke up with his last girlfriend because she related his personality to his sun sign characteristics; pisces. He hates the innacuracy of the word *amazing*, and he certainly didn't find anything cosmic or coincidental about bumping into Janet's family, so far from his home town in Florida.

We dangled our legs off a boulder and waited for our hearts to slow. Eventually, we took off our shoes and wandered back along the green, ancestral path. Was this grass descended from the same roots that grew here a thousand years ago? It's soft on the toes. A curious llama. Orange sunset. We dragged our palms along hand-carved walls.

Finally, all the tourists were bused off. It was just us and that postcard vision. He laid on his back in a patch of grass. I stared into the setting sun.

We tried to do what Machu Picchu would want us to do, nothing. Finally, a guard discovered us and in a quick flash of Spanish, kicked us out.

CROCODILE ISLAND

Havana, Cuba

"Ju like girls? Fuckin' hot Cuban girls, man? Ju like music? Buena Vista Social Club an shit? Yea! Ju like dancin', salsa dancin'! Oh yea, ju like dancin'! I see ju like dancin', baby! Where ju from?"

Rus: New York

"Oh Nueva Jork! Yea, man, I gotta cousin in Nueva Jork! Man he in Queens, bro! Ju know Queens! Where ju from?"

Rus: Brooklyn

"Oh yea, man, Brooklyn-Man! Fuckin' Jay ZEEEE 'n shit! Big-E! That shit's tight. What'chu want, man? Smokes, ladies, Mary Jane, fuckin' blow man, coke? Don't worry, I hook it up, man! I got yo shit! Ju jus tell me an' I got chu!"

I can talk like this for hours.

We crawl the inky Havana streets and I fake-hustle my buddy into wretched temptation. It was the only way we could get around Havana, day or night.

Jineteros, Cuba's street hustlers, are everywhere. They pop out of doorways and run a long con. They know where you sleep. They wait for you to finish lunch. These are the smooth, clingy, salesmen of the streets.

It goes a little something like this:

Hey, Hola! Where you from!

They hold their hand-shakable hand out. They keep it there, outstretched, hovering towards your heart. Patient. Finally, give in. You shake the hand.

Oh Nueva York! Yea! I gotta cousin/aunt who lives there!

Yea, right.

Welcome to Cuba, man!

How nice, you smile.

How ju like my country?

You lie.

How long ju gonna be here?

You approximate.

Ju like music?

Of course you do.

Buena Vista Social Club! Fuckin' salsa, right!

You've heard that album.

Ju wan cigars man? I got the good fuckin' Cohibas.
The real deal, man.

You don't smoke.

Ju like girls?

You like girls.

I got hot girls man! I make quick call. These girls are the hottest, bro!

Not those kind of girls.

Come inside here, man, let's have a beer! You seem cool, man!

No, thanks.

Why!? You don't like beer?

You like beer.

What ju don like?

You shrug.

Ok, I come walk around wit ju guys.

No, thanks

Ju guys come to my country and don't want to meet any people?

Yes. No. Sí.

Alright, whatever! Ju guys are fuckin weird, man!

You're angering the locals.

We breathe. Rus says he would have handled that more efficiently with more New York fuck-off attitude. We turn the corner.

Hey! Where you from!

Huge, welcoming smile, hand-shakable hand...

& again,
    & again,
        & again.

Separating Havana from the sea is the malecon; a cement barricade, a wide sidewalk and an 8-lane boulevard. Teens chatting in groups sit on the barricade: smoking, dancing, making out.

The light turned red. We crossed.

In the middle of the road, two people stood in our way. One was a muscular dude in drag, and the other was his stocky, black-dressed sidekick. The big guy was a head taller than me. He rasped, "Hey baby, ju look so gooooooood, lemme take you home. Where ju staaaaaayin'?"

Rus and I looked at each other painfully. Dammit. We'd stopped the jinetero schtick for 10 seconds to walk across the street.

The big dude hugged my arms powerfully down to my sides. I was pinned in place. He did a grindy dance move that only Latinos can do — he swirled his crotch while whispering some sexy garbage in my ear.

No, no, no. Thanks. I smiled, I laughed. What else could I do? I looked at Rus pleadingly. The guy had me pretty tight. I could smell his squishy, purple lips. The light was still red, but the countdown was getting close.

Rus shouted: "Girls! Please. He's mine!" He playfully pushed the huge dude aside and smacked my ass. He pulled my arm from my side, where the dude still had me gripped. We dashed across the street. I threw in a little skip move, for good measure. The light turned green. Cars from the 50's grumbled and groaned. Old engines muttered curses in español. We didn't look back.

At the far corner, I started my jinetero routine again immediately. "Ju like big dicks bro? Big, fuckin' thick, Latin cocks, mang?" Two *jineteros* who were heading towards us shrunk away.

Rus: Let's check the map.

DB: Ok — ah, shit.

While the big one held my arms, the quiet one had picked my pocket. The whole sex proposition was a ruse. Of course. What is more distracting than a six foot dude with lipstick doing a humpy dance in the middle of an 8-lane road?

Good thing that bulge in my back pocket had been a map. My money was safely stowed in my money belt, tucked into the front of my pants.

Bitches.

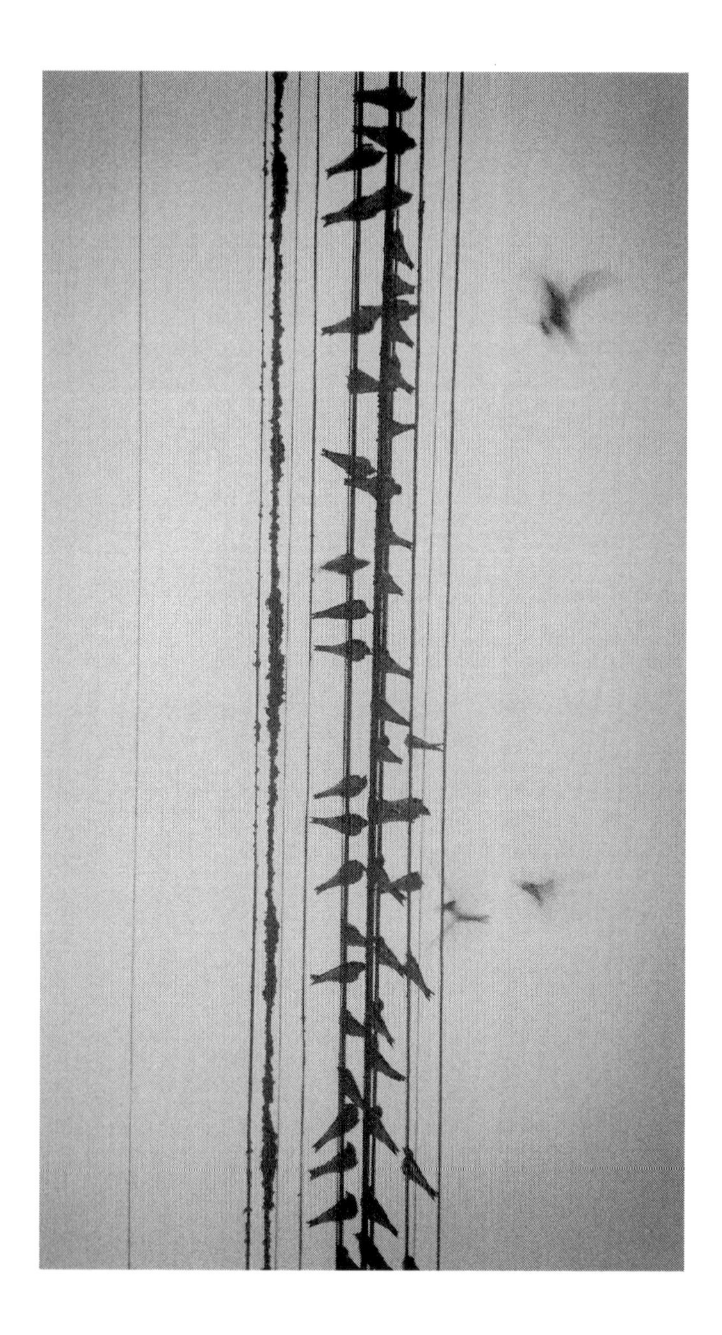

THE CROW WITH GOLDEN WINGS

A Korean Fairy Tale

A crow was born with gold-colored wings. His body was black, but his wings glittered and reflected the sun.

{ Freak! }

The other crows despised him.

His ostracism dug ruins into his mind. One day, he dove from a high branch and flew beyond his forest.

Uncountable miles.

Somewhere else.

A redwood emerged through the fog. A young bird was roiling in a pile of leaves. He drifted down and sat beside her.

{ I fell from that branch. My... It's broken }

The young bird barely whispered. Her wide eyes pointed up to the tree and down to her wing.

The crow plucked a golden feather from his wing and gave it to the injured bird.

Here.

As she held the golden feather, her broken wing began to mend. The two birds stared at each other. In seconds, they watched bones heal, muscles regrow and feathers form.

Can you fly?

The bird flapped her blue-black wings a few feet into the air. She looked down at the crow with the golden wings.

The golden-winged crow looked up at the hovering bird. He watched her circle and fly away. A warmth drifted into his body, something he had never felt.

He looked at the space in his wing from where he had plucked the golden feather. A black one had grown in its place.

A few days later, he noticed another wounded bird. Again, he offered a golden feather. A miraculous healing. A black feather replaced the gold.

Time spun forward at all speeds, imperceptibly.

The golden-winged crow gave his healing feathers to squirrels, mice, cats, bears and other creatures.

One day, he swooped down to a rock next to a badger with a broken tooth.

Here, take this.

He reached into his wing, but his golden feathers were gone. His wings were black. He looked like a crow.

{ Take what? }

I'm sorry. I… wish I could help you.

The crow stepped into the air. He didn't know what to do. After many sunsets, he recognized the forest of his youth. He curled his claws around a branch in the center of his old forest. One sat next to him. Another. Soon the whole flock gathered. They wanted to hear of his travels and his life.

{ It looks like you've finally grown into your wings. Tell us, where have you been? }

He wanted to tell them stories. But something was wrong.

Finally, I look like you. It took my entire life. I've given every feather I had.

His family of crows stood silent.

I'm not the crow who left here years ago. The places I've been… those I've shared my life with… they have made me who I am.

The crow who once had golden wings looked around him at the tree full of crows. Each of them with perfect, shiny black feathers.

I always wished I could be part of this flock. But I'm not like you all. I realize that I never was.

He lifted off the branch and flew out of his old forest with a quick swipe of his fresh, black wings.

FUCK IS EVERYTHING

Huanchaco, Trujillo, Peru

I stood there in front of the class; 30 cute Peruvian 10-year-olds smiling

! HOLA !

Hola! Soy Dany. My name is Dany. Soy un Norte Americano, de Nueva Jork. I'm from North America, from New York. Tu sabes Nueva Jork? Do you know New York?

Sí, sí!

Tengo un pregunta. I have a question for you. What... is your name?

Blank stares. A spitball arcs, wet, through the air. Classic.

What is your name?

Suddenly I don't exist.

What... (Smile) is your... (raised, suspicious eyebrow) NAAAAAME?

Three hands raise like tall grass.

Come ON! Como te llamas?

Is this a joke? M sees my face and intervenes with a quick "Dan, don't be a dick" look.

Como te LLAMAS?

Arms shot up. I'm teaching English by asking them questions in Spanish. Great.

I ask them one-by-one what their name is. I say nice to meet you. They smile because they don't realize how far back their lack of English is putting them. I rant in my own mind. I convince myself I don't think this way because I'm a dick from North America.

Manuel told us to meet outside on the cement playground where students pay fifty cents for a hand-sized styrofoam plate of spaghetti, fish and a plastic fork. A crew of boys approached nervously, like a dog approaches a picnic, asking permission with each step. They circled around us. M talked with them in rapid Spanish.

M, to me: Do you understand?

No.

M: They're asking what fuck means. They saw it on the Internet.

The boys perked up when they heard her say fuck to me. They stepped in closer, tightening the circle.

What did you tell them?

M: Nothing. I'm not going to tell them. They'll run off telling everyone I told them what fuck means.

What do you think it means?

M: I don't know... (her face stayed but her eyes darted over to mine)

Fuck is everything. How can you explain everything?

The closest boy heard me but didn't understand. I looked at them, finally. Rough, cool, eating ice cream. One a bit cleaner, one with a few stains on his shirt and a tougher
face, one clearly the leader. A standard group of boys from any country, looking to swear and break things. Which one was me?

The leader finished his ice cream as I fished through the hundred Spanish words I knew for ways to explain what fuck means. He threw the stick in the dirt.

M put her face near his and barked in Spanish. He picked it up, walked towards the garbage until he thought we weren't paying attention, and threw it in the dirt.

I didn't care enough to tell him.

THE LONG STRAPS

Barranco, Lima, Peru

Sometimes I walk around in cities with metal blasting in my headphones because the music rounds out the rough edges of bus engines, grinding construction sounds, car alarms; the thoughts of other people. I sneak into this bubble where I control the thrashing drums and I know what happens in the end.

I was walking back at an irregular hour so I texted Chris because even men don't know what other men do when they think they're alone.

`[ 4:32 PM ] Heading Home`

A snapping, metallic pop like old cars make when they fail to start.

I looked across the four-lane, tree-shrouded boulevard. A woman was half-fallen. Her legs had gone out but she was still gripping her long purse straps. She screamed in little bursts. A man in a black hoodie was dragging her by her purse with his left hand. His right hand was trying to aim his gun at her body.

Let go.

The gunman released the purse and the woman fell backwards onto the sidewalk. He turned and jogged diagonally, away from us. He moved sluggishly, as if running was too much effort. He tilted up the fabric of his hood.

A couple who happened to be crossing the street screamed and sprinted back the way they came.

I snapped a few photos and a video of the gunman jogging away.

The woman's male companion pointed at an edge of the sidewalk where the bullet had chipped off a crescent of concrete. He held up the bullet. At point-blank range, the gunman had missed. The women sat together and held each other.

I realized that Tool had stopped, so I hit play. The drums and screaming felt soothing. I walked home as a few Police motorbikes whizzed by, much too late. Luckily, Chris wasn't doing anything I wouldn't do — he was cutting carrots for a salad.

II

NAUSEA

THE MAGIC BARGE

Green Island, Taiwan

If you beheld the grace by which I can projectile vomit a healthy breakfast off the side of a sea vessel, you might say I'm a virtuoso. The siren song of the swaying of the deck enchants my innards into revealing their murky contents.

In the *Lonely Planet* guidebook, there's a black box around a special note from an experienced traveller. It's a warning for what he calls *The Green Island Vomit Barge.* As a seasoned boat-riding traveller, he cautions, the two most sea-sickening boat rides of his life were going to and returning-from Green Island.

Shit.

I had stumbled upon a video of Grant Morrison talking about using what he called sigil magik to manifest his desires. It was a cryptic, frightening talk which involved strange symbols, meditation and fire. Even Grant himself, shaved head, black leather jacket, Scottish accent, seemed like a impure source of information. His podium had devil horns. But I had no choice.

The morning of the boat ride I awoke in a tiny house on the coast of Taiwan. With the sound of the ocean as my backdrop, I began to create my spell:

Step 1: Write your intention in the present tense.

`I AM ON THE BOAT AND I FEEL FINE`

Step 2: Remove all vowels.

`MNTHBTNDFLFN`

Step 3: Remove repeating consonants.

`MNTHBDFL`

Step 4: Concentrate on your intention. Draw a symbol using the remaining consonants.

I drew a something circular, filled with zig-zag lines.

Step 5: Burn the symbol. Let the flame touch your hand so you can feel the heat of the fire.

Done.

We boarded the boat.

There was an outdoor deck on the second level with trash buckets for pukers like me. We held onto the railing and tried not to look at each other. We faced the sea. Some of us took selfies to distract ourselves. Others plugged in our headphones. I started doing math.

What's 12 times 13, I asked myself. Well, 12 times 12 is 144. Add 12 and that's 156. Ok? Ok.

What's 11 times 15? 10 times 15 is 150. Add 15 and you get 165. Next?

Like Rainman, my mind became a sea of numbers. The boat was cruising. A petit woman in a tan sundress vomited into her own mouth, ambled meekly to a plastic bin and spat down the side. Her wretched politeness!

13 times 9. 10 times 9 is 90. 3 times 9 is 27. 90 plus 27 is 117.

The boat was rocking. Our wake was white. Sea birds I assumed were all albatrosses floated overhead. My eyes stuck to the flat line of the horizon the way a dog watches you chew your stinky tofu. I did math like Good Will Hunting. Was it some magical derangement that made me concentrate like this? What's 15 squared? 200 plus 25 is 225.

Suddenly, Green Island was within view. A teenage dude spewed over the edge with a spluttering of limbs. His performance art. *Convulsion of the Seas.* Beats by Dre glued like purple earmuffs.

A landmass; a pile of green cotton balls grew steadily ahead. I turned my head and smiled just a few moments too soon. The floor spun upwards. I lost the horizon. Oh no!

"Ok, bro?" Justin asked. My face was getting hot.

I tried to say something and couldn't. I was so close! The smell of the puke buckets seared my nose. The deck was a marshland.

19 times 9! 19 times 10 is 190, minus 9 is 181. 181 minus 96! 96 minus 81 is 15, 100 minus 15 is 85.

I was desperate. I was A Beautiful Mind. I was what's his name. I was Einstein chalking equations on blackboards. I was an absent-minded professor.

The island was so close I could jump out and swim there. We were docking! I could see taxis swarming the dock. I would have to negotiate! How much to the center of town? 100? No! 200 New Taiwanese Dollars? He'll say 200, then I'll say 150, then he'll say 175. We'll make a deal.

Trees and cliffs and fluffy clouds. I made it!

Magic.

SUN DANCE

Pine Ridge Indian Reservation, South Dakota, USA

I'm on all fours at the edge of an arroyo, trying to stop the spinning. I'm mumbling, "this is an arroyo. Is this an arroyo?" I didn't know what an arroyo is, and for the sake of this story, I'm not going to look it up.

Behind me there's a circle in the high desert. Scrubby grasses and a long, flat horizon. Nothing, forever. This is the estranged land that George Washington's ancestors begrudged Sitting Bull's ancestors. This is the end of the frontier.

The circle is 70 yards around. The outer edge, where supporters bang drums and chant, is covered with pine branches. Some are dressed in leather and beaded ceremonial garb, looking like I'd expect drum-pounding Native Americans to look. Others look straight out of rough LA neighborhoods with backwards hats, hip-hop t-shirts, and chain wallets.

Lakota drumming is a steady, relentless pounding. One bang every half-second, repeated forever. No break-beat, no double-beat, no dropping of the beat. After thirty, forty minutes, it's completely hypnotizing.

Four of us had been invited to watch a sacred ritual: The Dance of the Sun.

Twenty nearly-naked warriors stand in a large circle facing inward, bronze skin smeared with white paint and streaks of blood. Puffy scars bubble their backs, shoulders and arms. This inner circle represents the spiritual realm. The warriors are giving blood to appease the spirits; so the spirits won't get hungry and take their loved ones.

In the center of the circle, a thin tree stands absurdly tall. It has been dragged here from somewhere else. Twenty feet up, the trunk forks into a V. Strands of colored fabric dangle loosely in the dry air.

A warrior steps into the circle and raises his arms out to his sides. A face-painted Medicine Man tiptoes over melodramatically. A man in a bird-mask jumps into a dance and streaks to the warrior's side, head making erratic, pecking motions. The Medicine Man pulls out a thin spike of wood from a leather pouch and jabs it under the flesh of the warrior's shoulder. In and out the other side, so it's weaved into his skin.

Somehow there is no blood.

The Medicine Man ties one end of a rope around the wooden spike and the other end to a heavy cow skull. He repeats the skin-piercing and skull-tying to the warrior's other shoulder. Then he jumps, howls long and wild like a dog, waves his arms and backs away.

The warrior's legs step around in a circular dance. The white ropes take on the centrifugal force of his spinning; the skulls raise from the ground. He's spinning faster. The pounding of drums is heavy and repetitive. The sun is getting hotter. He keeps spinning, with cow skulls pulling on the flesh of his shoulders. His eyes are lost in the cloudless, infinite sky.

I slowly raise my arm, snap three quick photos with my phone, and slip it back into my pocket.

The Medicine Man returns to the warrior and waves the skulls down with a long move of his arm. The warrior slows, stops, and remains entranced. The Medicine Man grabs the spike from his left shoulder and pulls it sharply down. It tears through. The warrior's skin, now raised and puckered-out, still doesn't bleed. He rips the other side. The warrior steps back into the circle, staring into the sky.

A second warrior steps forward. Having not eaten or drank anything in days, he wavers gently, his sweat like tiny mirrors of sun. The Medicine Man glides over, puts a crow mask on him and slides his arms into black wings.

The Medicine Man pierces the warrior's back four times with wooden nails and ties long strips of fabric from the tall tree around them. The string is pulled, pulley-style, over the V in the tree. With a sharp jolt, the warrior is hauled into the air. He dangles from his back piercings. His skin stretches like saliva. As he's yanked upwards, his body tilts forward horizontally. The drums pound incessantly. I feel myself going insane. Blood pours out across the tan flesh of his back.

He flaps his wings. He's spazzing erratically. It dawns on me that he's trying to rip the spikes out of his back.

The flesh tears and he slams chest-first into the dusty ground. His blood mixes with the earth. I sink to my knees. I'm too hot. I'm sweating. I need to get out of here.

I crawl away from the circle, towards a scrubby cliff. I drag myself to the edge. *Is this an arroyo?* I wait for my equilibrium. I'm aware only that I don't know what an arroyo is, and that I'm about to throw up.

Some segment of Native American time passes. I look over my shoulder at the circle of the spiritual warriors' inner world, towards the supportive outer world of drum players, towards my four white friends and our Native American guide who brought us to this ceremony. I vacantly stumble towards them, not really wanting to arrive. The drum sounds press heavily into me, making my legs shaky.

Suddenly, the warrior who had the buffalo skulls ripped out of his shoulders storms across the circle. He's going straight at my friends. He's insanely fast. The whites of his inky, wild eyes. I'm struck by the fearsome power of Native American warriors. The flesh of his shoulders is flayed out like open mouths. I can see the darkness under his skin.

"HEY!" He screams directly into the face of my friend Moses.

"Spirit told me that YOU were taking photos!"

"Hey, no. I wasn't taking photos."

The warrior turns to Chris D, shouting, "It was YOU!?"

"No, brother. My camera is here in my pocket, but I didn't take any photos."

I'm frozen a few feet outside the outer circle. He doesn't seem to see me. I'm barely standing.

Our Native American friend, Richard, steps between the warrior and Chris, arms in a soothing, downward-patting motion. "Brother. I told our guests, no photos. I've been here with them. There is no problem. These are our friends."

"Who was it!? *Spirit* told me!"

The warrior is shouting.

The drumming has stopped.

All eyes are on the four gringos and the fury of this warrior.

Richard: We will leave now, brother. No harm intended.

The warrior howls wildly, like a coyote in Richards face, then turns and rages off. Is he going to get the Medicine Man? The chief? *Shit.*

My friends slink back away from the circle, towards the car. I emerge like a tumbleweed.

Richard: He is not allowed to leave the inner circle! In the inner circle, he is communing with the spirit realms. It is very dangerous to break the protective barrier between the spirit realm and the realm of the living! No! He is safe and protected by the medicine men in the circle. But he can't break out like that, especially in a rage!

DB: I took that photo.

Chris: *What!*

DB: It was just too incredible. That guy spinning and those skulls and everything.

Moses: We almost got killed back there.

DB: Holy shit, I know. I'm sorry.

Richard: I should have told you the rules.

DB: Somehow he didn't see me. Maybe Spirit dragged me out of the circle and hid me by that arroyo.

We drove through the skinny dirt roads in silence.

Richard: I fear the young people are becoming like this now. They are wild and some of them are very angry. You have to understand, these men are warriors. Lakota men carry with them the defeat of their people. They lost the war. These are deep wounds, brothers.

At the edge of the reservation, we parked in the gravel lot of a decrepit bowling alley. We marched into the blue light, ordered cheeseburgers, and ate in the sound of pins being knocked down.

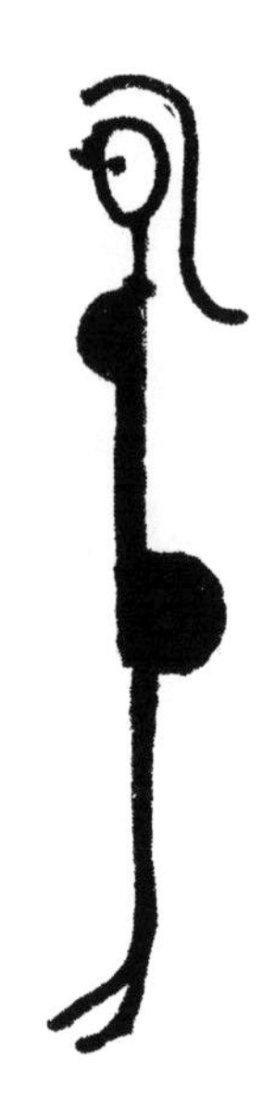

FAKE ASS

Guayaquil, Ecuador

I'd never seen a fake ass before.

M handled me staring and commenting about
this other girl's ass quite well, in retrospect.

She looked, hypothesized and concluded. Yes,
it must be fake.

It's like a tree trunk with a balloon stuck on.

To which she replied, Ok, that's enough.

I wasn't sure if it was part of the dress, some
hidden internal structure like shoulder pads.
Or was it surgically implanted?

I tried to stop thinking about it.

BURNING MIKE

Ramsey, New Jersey, USA

Cubby, the fat guy, burned Mike, the gay guy, with his cigarette.

Cubby was one of those brutes with thick-hands and cankles and you knew by looking at his eyebrows that he didn't have a reason. He was bigger than us and probably abused, but he shouldn't have put his cigarette out on Mike's hand.

If I had to guess, I'd say he was threatened by Mike's black nail polish and long hair; Cubby wished he could be thin and gay and free.

J, the bisexual guy, was hackey-sacking and heard Mike screech: *Ah-OW! What the fuck, man!?*

J attacked with sudden, effective violence. He appeared in front of Cubby like a panther, from nowhere. They did not talk about their feelings. His fist cracked straight into Cubby's lower jaw. His left leg snapped forward and smashed heavy in the center of Cubby's chest. As Cubby wavered, J's right leg roundhouse kicked him across the side of his head.

Three hard hits, three seconds. The sounds were different from movies sounds: thicker, flatter, sickening.

Cubby's knees met the grass. Another punch to the face and he laid back on the high school lawn with a wide-eyed, cloud-gazing look. J jumped on Cubby's chest and punched his face five times fast with alternating fists.

Cubby's friend edged towards the fight.

J stood up. His black shirt had a multi-colored, embroidered yin-yang across the chest that now dangled, tattered from its collar. He flexed the broken skin on his knuckles, glanced guiltily over his shoulders for an authority figure, and dashed off the school property.

Cubby didn't move.

Mike didn't move.

Nobody moved.

We stood in our little circles feeling the syrupy adrenaline work though our veins. Cubby's friend lit a cigarette and waited for him to recover.

ABOUT TURTLES

Ayampe, Manabi, Ecuador

She kicked a white piece of plastic away from the sea.

DB: What was that?

M: I'm just moving it away from the sea, so it doesn't go into the water and kill the turtles.

DB: Don't you think the waves will move up three feet in high tide?

M: I don't know, we use the metric system. I was just trying to save a turtle's life, ok?

DB: If you wanted to save the turtles you could have picked up the plastic.

M: Don't be a dick, ok? I was thinking about picking up the plastic and then I thought that there are no garbages anywhere and we were having such a nice walk so I just kicked it, I don't know.

DB: So you gave up on the turtles?

M: I just don't want to carry trash for half the day.

DB: There's a garbage can right there.

M: I didn't see that.

DB: You can go back and pick up that plastic and toss it in the garbage. We'll wait.

M: You could go back and pick it up, too.

DB: I could, but I don't give a shit about turtles.

M: How could you say that?

DB: At least I'm being honest. You're saying the same thing, just with your actions.

Juan: We all alike this, no? We want, we want, but don't do. We want other people do. We talk and walk and kick what we don't like.

We looked at Juan. He was tall and Colombian and had a mustache that was just long enough that the ends turned upwards, when it was windy, towards the sky. I nodded. M bit her lip. I didn't know he could speak English.

R01116 GA GA7 244 ADULT

18.00 GEN ADMISSION 18.00

3.00 NO REFUNDS OR EXCHANGES

GA SOUNDGARDEN

CA 5X * * * *

GA7 244 ROSELAND

OCW118A 239 W 52ND ST.,NYC

13SEP96 SAT NOV 16, 1996 7:30PM

THE BRIDGE

Manhattan, New York, USA

They were actually punching him in the face.

Fucking New Yorkers.
Bridge and Tunnel people.
Both.

Soundgarden just finished rocking the Roseland Ballroom. In the frenetic feedback of the *Jesus Christ Pose* encore, Chris Cornell raised his Les Paul over his head, and, with a howl, chucked it into the frothing arms of the mosh pit.

A Henry Rollins-faced fan snatched the guitar from the cigarette smog above our heads and hugged his tree trunk arms around it.

The crowd's arms reached in hungrily. The fan used his shoulders to fend off the groping. The strings stretched and snapped. The tuning knobs were ripped off. They snatched the volume knobs.

Someone kicked his legs out. He went down hard, flat on his back, arms still crossed over the guitar. The terrible, sticky floor. A memento mori.

The fan fought for it.

Faceless hands reached through bodiless legs to pry his fingers.

He was terribly strong. The jackals pulled and punched. The head of the guitar cracked. A black Doc Martin kicked his ribs. I watched his nose leak red across his cheek. He barked up at us from the floor.

An enormous security guard pushed his way through with a screeching police whistle. His beefy arms pressed us back.

An eye in the storm.

The fan's eyes widened. He stood up with his bloody face and pumped Chris Cornell's guitar above his head. He screamed at the empty stage, at the sky above. YEEEAAAAA!!!!!

I was proud of him. We all were, despite our madness.

The fan fought for something he wanted. I stood there like a camera.

The security guard listened to his earpiece, pursed his lips and shook his head. The fan's shoulders slumped. The security guard slowly, easily, slid the guitar from the fan's hands the way one might take a filet from a German Shepard; with a prayer.

I looked down. Something glimmered next to my Pumas. No one's head seemed to notice. I slowly, faux-unmotivatedly kneeled down without changing my shitty, eyebrow-knotted New Yorker facial expression. I was trying not to get mauled.

The bridge of a Les Paul is a dense, metal finger. It has two cuts that make it vaguely resemble a manta ray. It holds the tension of the strings. When the strings are removed, it falls off.

Of all the broken pieces, here was the best part. I slid it into my pocket.

Lights on.
Background music.
Where are my friends?

GARDEN STATE
PARKWAY

DADDY

Garden State Parkway, New Jersey, USA

Cans of Natty Light flipped and sprayed across the parkway.

U2's *Discotheque* was cranking out of our Jeep Cherokee as we smashed into the surprisingly spacious little trunk of the Nissan Altima that had slammed its brakes in front of us.

It was prom weekend.

The parkway had toll booths every few miles where drivers stopped and tossed change into yellow baskets. This particular toll booth came up all of a sudden as we sped up a hill. No time for brakes.

I moaned, *Duuuuuuuude!*

70 miles per hour of teenage testosterone, shitty music and tons of automotive steel cracked together.

It wasn't entirely our fault. The car in front of us had already rear-ended the car in front of them, and the car in front of them had already rear-ended the car in front of that. You can imagine what happened next.

BOOM!

A little red Acura impaled itself on our trunk. Then, unfortunately, screaming sounds.

Frozen in the fast lane in a river of smashed glass, plastic, and hissing beer cans. A black Honda slowed next to us. A high school kid with a ratty Yankees hat said *Yo, you OK?*

I was riding shotgun. S and I looked each other over with serious faces.

It didn't hurt.

We felt our legs, chests, peered back into the back seat. J seemed shaken, but she was putting her hair behind her ears. M, the French exchange student, looked unfazed, unimpressed, French.

DB: Yea, we're OK.

Cool. Yo, help us grab this beer before the cops come!

We hopped out. Grabbing cases of beer from the smashed cars and loading them into his Honda. Corona bottles, Bud cans, cases of Natty Light, Natty Ice. A plastic handle of Popov. Captain Morgan's.

We heaved arms full of beer and liquor back and forth from these 4 smoldering cars while other cars, speeding over the hill, swerved around us. The driver in the red Acura kept screaming. Her arm and face were bleeding and nobody was paying attention.

I asked the driver of the black Honda, "Heading to Sleazeside?"

Yea, the Winwood or some shit.

"Cool, we're in The Breezes."

Come say what up.

We waited there in this screaming, decaying line up for a while, then put our hazards on and bumbled to the right shoulder.

The hood of our badass 1995 Jeep Cherokee wouldn't close all the way, but only because the grill was dented up about an inch. The back hatch wouldn't snap shut, but also, it was dented about an inch.

We waited for cops to take our info, but the other cars, injuries, and underage possession charges had taken precedence. Nobody seemed to recognize that we were part of the mayhem. Maybe because we had only sustained two inches of damage.

S: Should we just go?

DB: I mean, how long do we need to sit here?

S: Let's just go.

We ambled off the highway at the next exit and found a little hardware store. We bought a roll of silver duct tape to tape the hood down and the back hatch shut. After ten minutes of taping, S stood back and surveyed his black Cherokee. The silver lining.

S: It needs something.

J was beginning to look unwell. Her face was draining and she was hugging herself.

DB: We should get there already.

S: We have to make this right.

S bit off a length of the silver tape and squatted next to the driver door. He taped and ripped, taped and ripped. The French dude smoked and looked at his marvelous silver watch face. I don't know what face I was making. S stepped back.

S: Perfect. Let's go.

We looked at the driver's door of the Jeep. In 750-point duct tape all-caps was one word: DADDY.

WORM

Stockholm, Sweden

I woke up gagging on a shoelace, which is unusual.
Something was crawling out of my throat.
It was a shoelace.
Why is there a shoelace in my mouth?
When did I last eat a shoelace?
I don't remember.
It's halfway down my throat.
I'm pulling it out for longer than I'd like.
I hope I don't snap it in half.
Jesus, I really ate a lot of this shoelace.

There. It's out I — oh. I think it's moving.

I stepped into the bathroom and snapped on the light.

It's a worm, oh god it's a pink worm the size of a garden worm perfect for fishing in lakes. From a fishing perspective, this worm was easier to find than digging in the dirt after a rain. But not emotionally easier.

"Chris! I'm sorry to wake you, but you really have to see this."

Chris mumbled himself awake, grumbled something in Swedish, and stumbled to the sink in his underwear.
The worm was slowly flexing it's muscles.

"Tapeworm, dude. We'll figure it out in the morning."

He turned back to bed.

"Ok," I said.

I put the worm that was not a tapeworm into a drinking glass. Can it climb? It just climbed out of my throat. I flipped the glass over it like a roach.

I laid back under my covers and imagined a family of worms pouring out of me like river salmon. I went incognito mode. I didn't want Google to know. My fingers were shaking. I was afraid to sleep.

When the sun rose, we went to the hospital.

The nurse was a hand taller than me. She smiled and wore wooden shoes. She was like a tall, Swedish Amélie. I could sense her quirky introversion. She said lightly, "can I take a look at the… animal?"

I handed her the plastic bag which contained my worm but had also been used for a loaf of Swedish bread.Damp bread particles clung to the insides, adding a dirty atmosphere. It wasn't moving anymore. Just laying around. Lazy worm.

Get your own goddam lunch now, worm.

The nurse reached two long fingers on the end of a long arm, like a crane. She held it at arms length. Was she flirting with me?

"So… what exactly happened?"

"I don't usually drink that much, but last night I had quite a bit of vodka,
and then tequila.
Several shots of tequila,
which is ironic,
I think it's ironic,
anyway, because
after we went to sleep at around 5, so, say 7,
I woke up because this thing was crawling halfway down my throat.
It could have been crawling IN, I suppose, which would be better healthwise.
Scarier, perhaps, though.
So we'd have to find the den or whatever their sort of house or hive is called... it would be somewhere in Chris' apartment.
But I've been traveling quite a bit,
eating street food,
basically making every poor dietary decision I could possibly make.
For two years.
It's probably that.
It's probably my fault, ultimately.
I take responsibility for the worm.
Do you think there are others?"

These beautiful Swedish people like sentinels, saving me. I felt gnarled like an old, twisted tree.

She glimmered. "Do you think, maybe, that you were hallucinating?"

"Yes, I mean, of course, I hoped that at first. I thought it was a shoelace. Then the shoelace turned into a garden worm and wriggled around in a sink, in the dark, in Sweden. Yes, I did think, or hope, actually, that I was hallucinating."

They laughed because we all didn't know what to say.

I said, "I like your shoes."

"Thanks. They're from... up north, in north Sweden. It's called, well, it's like the end of the earth."

"They've got good taste at the end of the earth."

I was dying and I was praying they'd save me. I was vomiting worms.

Another nurse led Chris and I through a metal door, and another, down a lonely hallway. She pressed a red button to unlock another, deeper door. The sound of other people slid away. Our footsteps echoed. The lights were brighter here. We stood in a little white room with a single, sterile bed. There were rubber boots lined up next to the door. We were in quarantine.

The door hissed closed. Chris and I looked at each other.

Chris explained, "we are in the room which controls the contagious diseases."

A thin radio with a vintage dial perched on the stainless steel shelf. The antenna was gone but I found a station with scratchy pop music. As long as I touched the radio, we could hear a teenage girl whining about a teenage boy. These fucking kids.

This is the song I die to.

A half hour ticked by while I held this radio, wondering if there was symbolic meaning to all this.

Another nurse came in and led us back. Was that a test?

There was a larger area with private square areas cordoned off by movable screens. Sick-looking people on hospital beds. Concerned-looking family members. I was sipping a coffee that Chris had bought for me. Should I not be drinking here? These people have contagious diseases.

Today, I am one of these people.

The tall nurse wheeled a cart over and said, "hey, can I take some of your blood?"

She tightened the rubber tourniquet and snapped some pieces together.

"Ok," she said, as she stabbed me. "Tell me. What is the world like?"

My blood poured out into little tubes.

"The world is a huge… wild, lovely… delicious place. Every single day is different. Unpredictable. I mean, look at us now."

"I'm jealous," she said.

The tourniquet loosened.

She labeled my blood and I sipped my coffee.

"Do you think it's fatal? I mean, are the worms going to take over my body?"

"Probably," she said.

The rubber soles of her wooden shoes were silent as she rose to her full height and walked away, tall and light.

III

LOVE

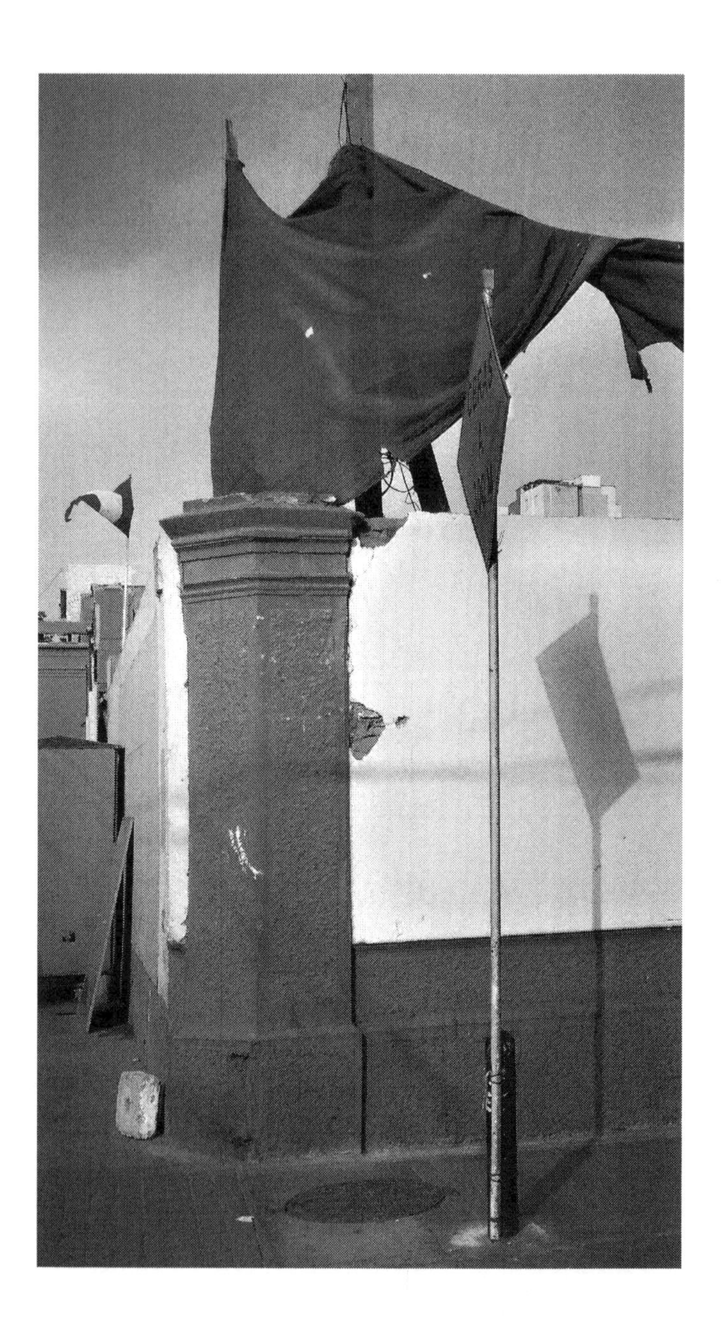

THE SUN

As Skyped to Dina

[7/17/14, 9:53:39 AM] DB: I had that perfect moment yesterday

[7/17/14, 9:53:57 AM] DB: They call it Lima the Gray because the sun doesn't come out

[7/17/14, 9:54:24 AM] DB: it always looks like its going to rain, but it never does, either.

[7/17/14, 9:54:38 AM] DB: It just stands at these points by the sea

[7/17/14, 9:54:58 AM] DB: For an hour or so, after lunch, the sun made the city glow

[7/17/14, 9:55:03 AM] DB: it didn't come out all the way

[7/17/14, 9:55:08 AM] DB: the sky didn't turn blue

[7/17/14, 9:55:32 AM] DB: but it was bright and warm and people like me slowed their New York walking with purpose pace

[7/17/14, 9:56:18 AM] DB: I stood by a street corner; there was a large, long, cement rectangle full of potted plants. A municipal installation of greenery.

[7/17/14, 9:56:22 AM] DB: A perfect bench

[7/17/14, 9:57:21 AM] DB: I sort of spun around and picked the best view of the sky above the buildings; above a construction site, a Peruvian red and white flag drooping and waving behind a street sign

[7/17/14, 9:59:10 AM] DB: My body reached a subtle posture just before I was sitting; that overlooked moment where the ass is hovering too low to be standing, and a bit above the bench. I was committed. I looked up.

[7/17/14, 9:59:16 AM] DB: A woman.

[7/17/14, 9:59:39 AM] DB: She had committed to the same spot, the same bench, the same pool of sunlight.

[7/17/14, 10:00:00 AM] DB: Our asses waved hello to one another, and then our faces

[7/17/14, 10:00:38 AM] DB: God I need the sun, she said in Spanish

[7/17/14, 10:01:01 AM] DB: Si, yo también, I replied.

[7/17/14, 10:01:44 AM] DB: We were sitting too close to act casual. This is the rim of a potted plant.

[7/17/14, 10:03:18 AM] DB: Her name is Maryori, like the month of March or May; from Medellin; she's here for a month to take care of her father and to learn English.

[7/17/14, 10:03:32 AM] DB: As her eyes began to take me in, she became self conscious.

[7/17/14, 10:03:49 AM] DB: I'm in my pajamas, she said and covered her face

[7/17/14, 10:04:15 AM] DB: Here's my number, she said. Let's get coffee, and then after that, let's drink.

[7/17/14, 10:05:19 AM] DB: She said something about how interesting it was that we both are here for a month, both to learn each other's language, and then in this sunny spot, how perfect

[7/17/14, 10:05:45 AM] DB: I was nodding; of course I had already realized these things.

[7/17/14, 10:05:48 AM] DB: xox

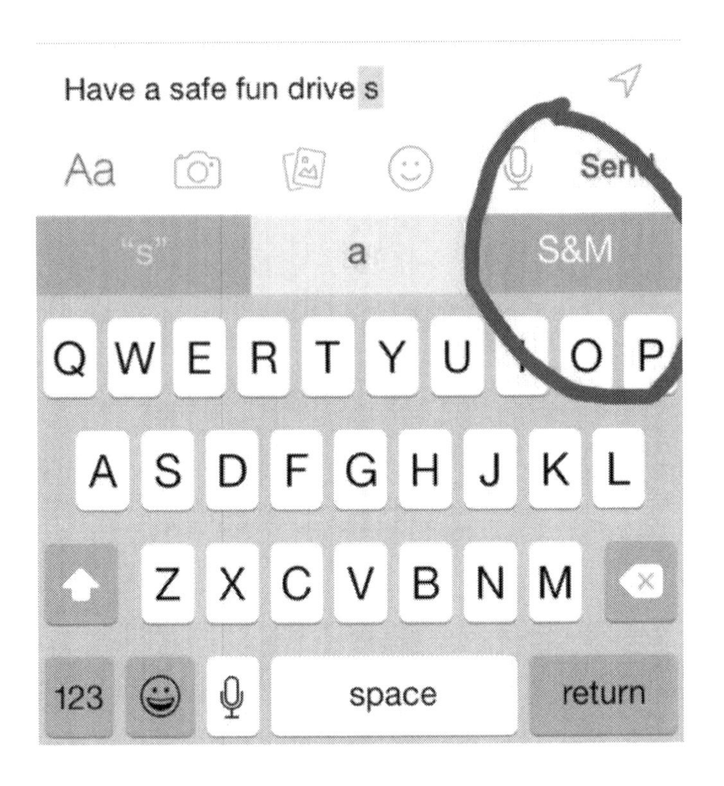
Have a safe fun drive s
Aa
Sen
"s"
a
S&M
Q W E R T Y U I O P
A S D F G H J K L
Z X C V B N M
123
space
return

S&M

I've never tied anybody up,
never clipped anything to my balls,
never worn anything made of latex,
never got a boner when someone whispered "you piece of shit",
never been chained to a wall by my piercings,
never electrocuted anyone sexually,
never held a horse whip,
never Googled S&M,
never even worn leather pants.

And yet, every time I type the letter S into my phone,
it predicts that I'm going to type S&M.

I know a man who shoves a horse tail in his ass and has his wife ride him around his living room. Or maybe his wife wears the tail in and he rides her. I never even asked.

I searched for signs of S&M through my hard drive, my email history, everything. Only one email from a year ago, Tom makes a joking comment about a CouchSurfer friend who's name is "S". He says:

```
No, haven't found S&M yet. might be better
trough FB. Man, that search function in CS
sucks balls
```

Day-to-day, I don't think about people crawling on all fours, begging for mercy or handcuffs or shiny black thongs, dildos, people putting cigarettes out on each other's ball sacks, teeth biting rubber gags, metal surgical tools. Maybe you do, and that's cool.

But since I upgraded my phone, I think, for half a second, twenty times a day, about these things because those two capital letters standing guard on either side of that naughty, twisty little ampersand: S&M. Those two letters are gonna make that bad little preposition pay for being such a dirty little symbol. Isn't that right you worthless little pretzel? You're not even a word. You're just a disgusting little curly cue pretending to be a word.

* whipping sounds, muffled screams

TELL ME A STORY

Huanchaco, Trujillo, Peru

I say, *Tell me a story.*
She says, *I can't. You tell one.*
I say, *Come on, tell me about today.*
She says, *I'm not good at stories.*
I say, *Ok, but you're telling the next one.*

> I laid there on my favorite spot on the beach.
> That little nook where the sand is carved out and it makes a perfect pillow for my head.
> My silky, oily, lusciously tan legs glistened erotically in the sun.

She laughs and punches me in that soft way.

> He said he was going to eat and come right back,
> but he's taking forever.
> Finally, I picked up my phone to message him, and there he was, smiling and flip-flopping towards me.
> He knelt. Touched my hair. Kissed my neck.
> He laid beside me and I curled around him.

Her gentle breathing sounds.

> We laid like that, my head rising and falling with his chest.
> The wild sea.

He had that faraway look.
I asked, What are you thinking about?
He said, *I'm trying to remember this moment.*
So I can come back here any time.
No matter what happens.
I laughed a bit. What a strange dude.
I wrapped my legs around his leg. I'm the scissors.
He's the paper.
Tiny rocks beneath us.
I feel magnets inside us, pulling us together.
There are forces out here in the breezy day pushing us together.
This person I barely know. The things I want to say.
I don't know the words in English.

Her eyes are blinking. She says, *How do you remember everything?*

His fingers drift across my skin.
A dusty, gray cloud slides across the sun.
We are becoming one thing.
There are waves behind waves, three, four layers crashing sequentially.
Suddenly, I had to pee. "I have to pee," I said.
We gathered our few things and I think he carried me all the way home.

She says, *Don't look at me.* She's laughing, hiding her eyes. Her fingertip whispers a heart across my shoulder.

She can't say it yet.

FISHING

Taipei, Taiwan

Fishing, she says. *You fished me.* She makes a hook with her finger and tilts her chin up. Smiles. *You're good.*

"I hooked you? Then I hooked us both. Are we hooked on different hooks? Or the same hook?"

What are you saying?

"I don't know. You said something about fishing."

Are you going to let me go? Or keep me?

"I'm definitely going to eat you."

I don't believe you. You say everything too perfectly.

That laugh where she hits my chest. She bends over and lets it wash over her. She wraps her hair behind her ear.

"I miss you already."

See? Too perfect. I don't believe.

My stomach hurts. I feel sick. I can't get up and face… you getting on a plane. "What if I never see you again?"

Oh, Dan. 5 more minutes. Let's look at photos of yesterday.

She hands me my phone. We're standing on a marble canyon. She's posing in front of a National Palace. A photo of an ugly baby; we laugh. We're climbing a mountainside on ancient stairs. We're smiling in temple ruins. Our cheeks pressed together, we fill the screen.

"You can still miss your plane. Let's go down to..."

Kenting?

"Yes! To the beach. We can figure out everything from there. Go anywhere. Do anything."

I kiss her cheek and think for the thousanth time how perfectly her features curve and slice and become her face. She looks into my right eye, then my left; back and forth every few seconds. I follow her. Somehow it's easy for me to look into those eyes. A pain in my chest.

"I'm gonna miss your face."

Is that the only part? She says, *let's go.* She's already told me that she's never been in love.

As we slide down together onto the bus stop bench, the airport bus arrives. Taipei traffic washes over us. The ticket-seller points to the bus, to us, and says something in Mandarin.

She hunches over her knees, away from me. Her long fingers touch her chin. She's frozen in time. Maybe that's my super power, I think. Freeze her in time.

The bus door closes. The ticket-seller makes a running motion with her fingers and points at a laminated schedule. The next bus is in 15 minutes.

She still doesn't move. Her fingers drum her knee. Two black-painted fingernails, three with glitter on black.

She tells me how she told someone that she has a boyfriend just to kill his creepy advances. I smile and say, "Oh, a boyfriend... you mean me? In the future?"

She's suddenly all huge eyes above that mischievous smile.

You want? You can.

This moment isn't fair. Now we're in traffic, a bus coming, and she's wide open. I panic; the sugar coating she says I do disappears. I almost yell.

"I don't know if I'll ever see you again!"

Those are her words. Our fears. She sees that I'm as lost as she feels. Her eyes follow her head down. Arms cross fast across her cross-legged lap.

I backpedal. My voice is high and terrible.

"Yes, of course I want to. I want to be with you. But how will it work? Let's talk about it. If you get a place in Seoul, I'll be there. Get a job in Barcelona and call me. Yes! I want."

But she's not listening to me anymore.

I think that's the last thing we say to each other. The next bus comes and she stands to let me hug her. Her legs aren't moving. The passengers load their bags and sit down. The bus door closes in front of her. The ticket-seller yells something in Mandarin and the door re-opens. She steps into the bus and though I hope she will, she doesn't look back.

WARNING
SWITCH MUST BE TURNED OFF BEFORE
OPENING FUSE DOOR. CLOSE FUSE
DOOR BEFORE TURNING SWITCH ON

MY OLD, EX, WONDERFUL FRIEND

My ex girlfriend.

I realize most of my girl : friends are

I broke up with her regrettably She is my most charismatic girlfriend

Most like able

She kisses her friends when she arrives and when she leaves; mostly on the lips.

We made love on the beach in Portugal, on the train in Switzerland, after Bolognese in Bologna, a bathroom in Marrakesh. Her brother never liked me.

She messaged me last night:

`So... I have to tell you something...`

Which either means she's pregnant or dying; I predict.

What else does that mean?

That type of abuse of people's focus and energy.

It's been 31 hours since she sent it.

Cliffhangers.

VOLCAN GRANDE

San Cristobal, Galápagos, Ecuador

The taxi was supposed to take us to the beach. Why were we stopped in a drizzly parking lot?

The taxi driver pointed out the passenger window towards a trail that led into a thick fog. "You walking up. *Es volcan grande.*"

"How is it up there?" I called to four French tourists who were mounting their bicycles.

"We see nothing. We are biking two-and-half hours like zis—". He tilted his hand at a hellish diagonal. "And at ze top—". He blew out the front of his lips, which, in French, means *I ain't seen shit.*

The mist was wet and clingy. We were inside a cloud. We decided to do it anyway.

The steps were half-steps and wet which made the climb awkward and slippery. We laughed and shivered into the dense gray atmosphere.

Our shoes were soaked when we got to the rim. A short path led down into the caldera, and ended in a small, wooden platform. The French guy was right, we couldn't see much.

"Is that a duck?" She said

DB: Yes. That's what we get. The edge of this lagoon, the gray mist, and one duck.

"Hmmmm..." She said.

DB: I love it. Wow. It's perfect. It's all mysterious and—

"We should have sex."

DB: Ok.

"Wait, should we, really?"

DB: Sex in a volcano, in the Galápagos? Yes, of course.

I started to un-velcro my shorts.

"What if somebody comes?"

DB: They'll see something worth the hike.

She laughed, bent forward, and put her hands on the railing. I did the rest.

THE HEART BEARS THE BEATING

It
Builds like fire working through me
Like I have no choice
The heart bears
the beating

//

DRAGONFLY

Luang Prabang, Laos

I sat facing her.
Drinking lassies
at different tables
at an Indian joint
in a Laos town;
an ex-French colony.

Tourists wearing tiny red dresses or blooming elephant-printed zoomba pants. I think that's what they're called, those parachute pants that musclemen used to wear.

She stood up, possessed.
I thought her lassie had turned on her.
Or maybe the Mekong river had seeped into her toothbrush last night and she was going to shit herself in the road in front of all of us broken-hearted lovers, sweating, shopping, waiting for something.

Her arm moved in slow rainbows, then the other arm.
Her bizarre dance. She turned to me and smiled.
A dragonfly hovered above a white sedan.

Do you see it?
Yes.

I saw the string.

A single strand of spiderweb entwined with the wing of the dragonfly, and like a dog on a chain — the dragonfly could only fly so far.

Did I get it? she asked me.
No, it's still stuck.

I sipped my banana lassie. She was perfect, then.

Not yet! I urged. *There!*
The dragonfly zipped into the sky.

That was heroic, I said and sipped. The heat was draining.

Wait! It's back?

The dragonfly, after seven seconds of ultimate freedom, had returned to hover in the space just above the trunk of the car.

We watched it together, not sure what to say to each other. Her, the rescuer and hero; me, her biggest fan.

A second dragonfly whipped down!
Then, two dragonflies,
dueling,
chasing,
figure eights.
Infinities!
It only took seconds, then
into the sky.

OIL

Somewhere between Tallinn and Tartu, Estonia

18 km left

We were going to run out of gas.

Not if… but where.

Should we turn back and run out of gas closer to Tallinn? Or should we keep going and run out of gas hoping to find a gas station?

17 km left

That was fast.

16 km

Should we hope? The TomTom GPS that should burn in hell said there were two gas stations right… there. And there. In those empty fields of Aspens.

15 km

Rene said, "is that… something?" An 18-wheeler covered our view. I let up on the gas. Stupid automatic rental car. How do I conserve gas with this thing? A car came up fast behind us, stayed for a moment then went around. I said, "that was nice. He didn't even honk or flash his lights."

Rene said, "They don't honk in Estonia. They follow you home and kill your family. He is now driving to find your girlfriend."

14 km

No gas station. Dammit, just a house.

13 km

I said, "it will be a good story. Starving and freezing to death on the way to a book reading. Would we resort to cannibalism?"

Rene said, "this is Estonian fairy tale."

12 km

We exited into a recreated Viking village, off a side road to a smaller road, to a smaller road, following a sign for a restaurant.

11 km

Let's not die in the cold on an empty stomach.

10 km

9 km

8 km

We coasted towards a proper white house and stormed inside. Two couples sat near a crackling fireplace. One couple was sharing soup. The other was holding each other's faces and making out.

Sitting at the bar was a charming-looking woman wearing pointed eye glasses that smart people wear. Rene asked her something in Estonian.

"She says there is a petrol station 12 km from here."

She wrapped a blanket around herself and said, "he said you're on a book tour. What book?"

"Ma Tapsin Roti," I said, trying to speak Estonian.

"What?"

"Ma Tapsin Roti? I Killed a Rat."

"I've heard of that!"

"Really?"

She picked up her phone, and there was my face, glowing in the screen. Rene handed her a book.

"You have to… sign it," she said. "My name is Kati."

"With a Y or an I?"

"I doesn't matter."

Two women came out of the kitchen. One, sturdy, in an apron, who shook my hand courteously with a little nod, and a mousey, ice-colored waitress.

Kati said, "this is Svetlana. She used to manage a… how you say… happy ending massage parlor. Now she is our chef. This is Inge. She is just out of school, so we are teaching her about life."

"And you?"

"I'm perfect, except for one thing. I hug."

While Rene and I ate our lunch, Katy read Ma Tapsin Roti to these two women. The translucent waitress folded her arms and looked at the sky. Svetlana leaned against the bar and twisted a towel in her hands.

I wanted to never leave this moment. I wanted to hug them and run out of gas here and be happy in this peaceful place. My stories had life without me. They were being passed, person to person. I wanted to get a nice, oily hand job for the road but there was no time.

Katy gave us her number and said she'd pick us up if we got stranded. It didn't matter anymore if we ran out of gas. We'd already made it.

SEA CREATURES

San Cristobal Island, Galápagos, Ecuador

I opened the our black beach bag and dumped out two snorkels, two masks, four flippers, and a frayed, orange towel.

Ahead of us, a dozen rocky steps led down to a thin, concrete path and a little jump into the sea.

We were alone.

I said, "I'm honored to be with you for your first snorkeling adventure, ever."

"What does that mean?"

"I don't know, I was just trying to say something nice."

"Are you sure there are no sharks in there?"

"People swim here every day."

"If we see a shark, I'm going to die. Immediately."

"Well, it has to bite you first."

"Alalalala! Stop!"

"Usually, sharks are only attracted by the scent of blood. So unless you're bleeding, or it's that time of the month—"

"Please… shut the—"

"Because then we'd be leaving a trail of blood that will be like candy for sharks."

"I'm not going." She crossed her arms. Why was I teasing her?

"What do you mean you're not going?"

"I don't want to be leaving a trail of bloody shark candy! I told you. I'm scared! The ocean! I don't know what's in there. I can't do it."

"Come on, get your snorkel."

"No!"

"I'm just giving you the standard, healthy dose of fear that every snorkeler has when they dive into shark-infested waters."

We pressed our masks onto our faces and squeezed our feet into the stiff black flippers. Our snorkels slid up into the rubber headbands.

"I'm shaking," she said.

"This place is incredible."

A black, volcanic ridge rose sharply from the back of the eyeball-shaped swimming hole. A pair of blue-footed boobies perched and waddled; our oblivious audience. A lizard the size of a man's leg sunned itself prehistorically on a rock. The subtle waves pressed inwards on the sunset-colored crabs who hunkered down or tiptoed to avoid the tides.

We were ready.

She flapped towards the water. It's an awkward thing, watching a sexy woman waddle in flippers, her perfect bikini ass below a bulging snorkel face. She didn't wait.

I was fumbling with my phone when a huge, male sea lion leaped out of the water and belly flopped on the path ahead of her. It's voice was like a huge burping and it belched at her angrily. Her hands pulled up to her chest and her elbows pulled inwards— she does T-Rex arms when she's scared. She screamed, then yelled in Italian. It barked back. She made the Italian hand gesture for keep moving. It leapt towards her like a blob. It's two little flippers barely held it upright. It propped itself up and started hurling itself towards her, fast. She screeched and jumped off the path onto a jagged volcanic shelf.

The sea lion roared at her, then lunged towards me. Shit. Can these things climb stairs? It's screaming, whiskered cheeks curled around fierce, yellow teeth. I had not learned the necessary... anything about sea lions. I backed up a few stairs.

The sea lion seemed to be howling territorially this is my house! Get out of my house! Then he flopped down, closed his eyes, and exhaled dramatically.

M yelled at him, "really!? Is this really necessary?"

We looked at each other, at the sea lion, back at each other. What to do?

Her worries were intensifying. "I think we're trespassing. Once we get in the water, he's going to attack us. This is his… spot."

As if on cue, the sea lion barked to life and lunged towards me, then flop-ran back down the path. He looked at her, paused, then tipped over the edge of the sidewalk, into the sea.

She hopped back onto the path and I waddled to her.

"Now he's in there, too," she said, and pointed to the bluest, most inviting swimming hole imaginable. A white cloud stretched elastically across the blue horizon.

I said, "only one thing to do."

She shook her head, "I can't now. It's too many things. Sharks. This asshole sea lion. Huge lizards. And the sea! I can't."

"Wait. Let me video that. Ok, say it all again. Why can't we go snorkeling in… this epic, exotic, perfectly blue lagoon?"

"Stop. Put your stupid phone away." I was bluffing. I was scared now, hoping she'd turn back, so I could, too.

She knelt down, eased her flipper feet into the sea, pressed off the rocks and slid into the water. Just like that.

I stashed my camera in a rock crevice and prayed an iguana wouldn't pry it loose. She was already a school bus length ahead. I dove down so she would see me coming from below.

A table-sized turtle drifted past us close enough to touch. It glided away from us, towards a shaft of sunlight. She squeezed my arm to share it's silent grace.

She popped her head out of the water. "I'm so fucking scared," she gasped. The sea lion burped from the distant shore. Her snorkel hung to the side of her mouth. She pushed her goggles up and wiped her eyes. "Shit shit shit!" Her head was bobbing up and down erratically. Her legs must have been kicking like crazy down there.

Then she pulled the goggles down and pressed the center into her forehead to squeeze out the air.

"Do you want to go back?" I asked.

"No." She tilted forward, grabbed my arm and pulled me deeper.

DONDE LA MER

San Sebastián, Spain

I don't usually share bathroom stalls with strangers. But this guy whispered *¿Amigo, quieres un poco de cocaína?*

Hell, I thought, I'll try anything four or five times.

I burst out of the filthy little room, onto the Cuban-themed dance floor and started shaking my ass, which, I decided then, is only fun while high. I can't get it up and don't have the attention span to conversate — but dancing with strange women in that window of super-hero time — this cute British girl slid my fedora onto her head and we're bumping, grinding, smiling, making out — she wants my email and I shout over the music WHAT'S THE POINT? WE'RE NEVER GOING TO SEE EACH OTHER AGAIN! I try to follow that up with another kiss because honesty should slice through all things. I'm cokehead Honest Abe. I'm Pinnoccio's stubborn wooden nose. Her hips stop and her nose wrinkles and I think she says *fuck off* but I'm smiling and I've got my friends behind me — it goes dark for a second, my hat is back on.

The dancing continues and then the fiending begins. The nice guy is gone. Both within me and the guy who offered me coke in the bathroom. We search for more. These Aussie girls and I. Nothing. They drift back to our hotel. Rus goes back to our hotel. I should go back, I know. I keep saying it to myself and even to this American dude who is smoking Camels outside and wearing florescent orange Wayfarers. It's 3am. I tell him I should go home, again, just to be sure I'm speaking out loud.

After party, bro. Come on. It's just a little walk.

Sweet, I say.

We walk and walk, and it seems like forever. The cozy light of the old city fades behind us and we walk out to a part of the sea that I hadn't seen. He slides his shades off to show me a black eye.

You should see the other guy.

Yea, I say.

That subtle paranoia. We walk farther than my sense of direction. We're on a sidewalk along the edge of the beach. Construction walls to the left. Dark sand to the right. A cop is walking towards us.

Don't worry, bro. I speak español.

Ok, I say.

The cop approaches us seriously. My amigo is too friendly. He is touching the cop's arm and smiling exaggeratedly. For some reason that may have been established in español, we turn 180 and begin walking with the cop. I don't like this. What is an American wearing sunglasses have to talk to a cop about at 4am? What the FUCK are they talking about? I can't reel my mind in. I'm not going to jeopardize my freedom for this little fucker. I start walking faster. I'm ten yards ahead of them. I look back and they're using more body language. I don't think the cop likes all the touching. Shit. I know I'm paranoid. I know I should have gone home. I don't have anything on me. The construction wall ends in a few yards.

I'm going to break for it.

I get to the corner. I turn it sharply. I kick off my flip flops and burst into a full sprint. I'm running as fast as a barefoot human on drugs at 4am running from Spanish cops can run. I'm a blur. Street lights and parked cars streak by in warp speed. My feet slap the pavement like a rainstorm. I remember that running on the balls of your feet is, I don't know what, but I remember it, and do it and it's the reason why I can only hobble for the next two days.

I take a turn and then another and another until there is no way that cop and that undercover bastard with the fake sunglasses can track me.

Shit, I'm in the suburbs.

Google is not here with me. I don't have any devices to orient myself. I know San Sebastián is banana-shaped; sea on both sides. If I can find the sea, I can make my way to the old city; if I get to the cobblestone roads, I can find the hotel.

A woman steps cautiously out of her townhouse into the pre-dawn light. Smartly dressed, ready to greet the work day. I gallup up to her. Shit, I realize as I open my mouth. No habla español. 10 years of French classes. What's the sea? *La Mar? La Mer!*

DONDE LA MER! The words burst out of my face. DONDE

LA MER? I try to calm down.

She power-walks to her car. I watch her like that sad part in the middle of a movie where she walks away and he stands there. The ignition snaps on and she speeds away. What the hell?

I'm wearing a button down shirt dammit. I'm respectable!

I sprint somewhere else, hoping to the sea. A man! He's in his car but the window is open. I try not to surprise him, but I scream DONDE LA MER! DONDE LA MER, SEÑOR!

This is an easy goddamn question for someone who lives in a beach town. He zips up his window and his little European smart car putters off. He didn't even look at me. What the HELL?

I'm being punished. I'm sorry mom. I don't know why it ends like this, stumbling barefoot. I don't know how I got so far off track.

A woman walking her dog. DONDE LA MER! POR FAVOR! LA MER LA MER! I'm pointing like a scarecrow. I'm on the yellow brick road. I'm giving her a clue. Just point! Please. See how easy I can point? My arms, your arms! The international body language of arms! She looks at me for a full second and walks on, staring harshly at her dog.

I'm confused. This is Myst. Where in the World is Carmen Santiago? This is King's Quest. I run through the streets variously. The sun rises. Somehow I curve around a stone church and my feet sense smooth cobblestones. The ancient streets of San Sebastián are as wide as a garbage truck. Tight corners, twisted cul-de-sacs lined with charismatically decaying six-story buildings. A sense of direction. The hotel.

"Rus!" I scream over and over at the brick façade. He dangles his head out of the second story window. "I don't have a key!" I croak.

"Danny! Jesus, what happened? You look like shit! Where are your shoes?

"Rus! I got lost! I've been shouting *donde la mer* and these fuckers won't even look at me."

"What won't they tell you? Where is the shit?"

"La mer! La mer! The fucking SEA! The ocean, the MER! Isn't... that the sea?"

Rus: It sounds like your saying MIERDE. Your accent is terrible. You're saying 'where is the shit', basically. That's why they're not looking at you. Dan, you're confusing these people. Where are your shoes?

"I had to run so I kicked them off."

Rus: So you've been running barefoot, with that stain on your shirt, shouting where is the shit for the last four hours.

"Dude! Let me up!"

"Sorry, D. I have a shoes and shirts policy. I really can't."

"I don't think I'm going to be able to walk tomorrow."

"And it's *donde está EL mar.* Try saying that real quick, for next time.

"You fucker. *Donde el mar?* OK?"

"It's right over there."

He pointed.

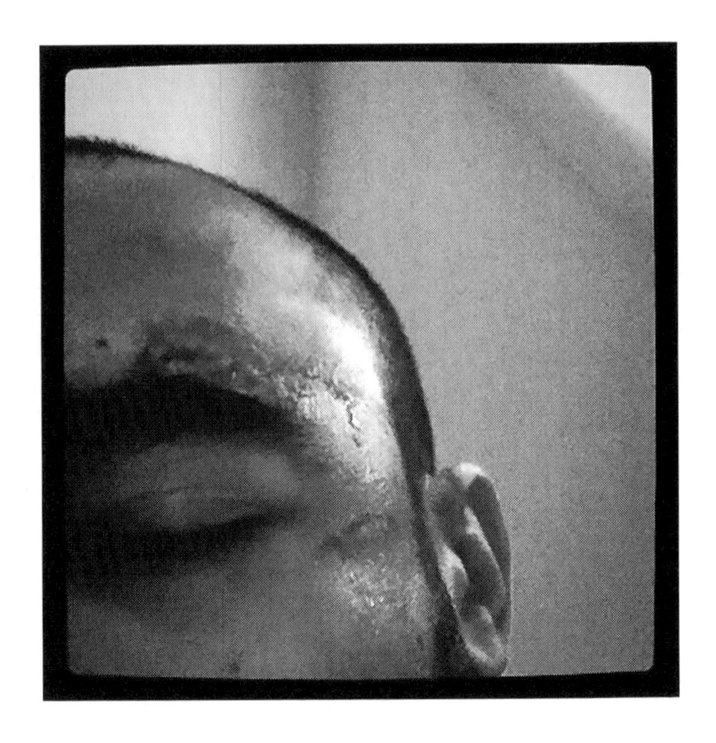

MOUNTAIN TREE COW

Boulder, Colorado, USA

I only know so much about Mahākāla.

If you're unable to attain enlightenment by the normal means such as meditation, fasting, being a good person, etcetera, Mahākāla chases you there with wretched, bloody heads. You'll be scared shitless and you'll run because people run from scary things. Then you'll burst through into sweet, bright enlightenment. Whatever that is.

Mahākāla is the scariest, most loving god of all.

//

On Cinco de Mayo, we celebrated Mexican independence by washing down pork tacos with pitchers of strong, zesty margaritas. Then back to my place for whisky cocktails and hallucinogenic mushrooms before ambling down the block to see the Black Angels rock the Fox Theatre.

The extreme volume and hypnotic strobe lights sent our psychologist friend out to hide in the deli across the street, fearing that his brain would be tricked into an epileptic fit. I was dancing like a madman, puffing joints from the Coloradans to my left and right. JF bopped next to me, a gentle smile simmering.

Encore! This might be the best, loudest concert I've ever seen.

Then! A wave of nausea. *Shit!* I signaled to JF, *I'm heading to the bathroom.*

On my way to puke somewhere, I tripped up a short set of stairs, smashed my forehead on the floor and knocked myself unconscious. The skull bone above my left eyebrow ripped through the skin to enjoy the dark, smoky air. Fragments of teeth on my tongue. I laid there, bleeding, for an undetermined amount of time.

A friend of a friend stumbled over my body, dragged it outside to the curb, and notified the ambulance across the street.

A spinning, awakening. An EMT with an angry cop voice was, I think, grilling me: *"SIR!* What is your name? Do you know your *name?* Do you know—"

"I'm fine." I muttered and swayed. I rose from fetal to crawling position. "I just fell hit my head I'm fine. I'm just walk home. I'm fine, fine. I'm fine." I vomited on the roots of a sapling that was growing through the sidewalk.

EMT: Sir, please sit down. *Sir!*

I was weaving and wavering and puking on a tree like a true goddamn drunk. There was no way to convince the EMT that I was ok. Dammit. I sat down.

Suddenly, I woke up as if from a sit-com nightmare, gasping, sweating, sitting up straight. Unbearably bright lights blew out my vision. This is bad science fiction. This is how you disappear. I've been abducted by the secret whatever people from the government thing. *I don't know!* Bad bad. I need to get out of here.

Loud serious voice: *Sir,* please lay down.

DB: YOU'VE GOT THE WRONG GUY! Let me *out!*

EMT: Sir! Lay down!

DB: You gotta let me go! I didn't DO ANYTHING!

EMT to another EMT: Restrain him.

Deft as a machine, they velcroed my arms and legs to the board I was laying on, strapped my chest down, snapped my neck into a medical dog cone and tied that to the board as well. It took about seven seconds.

DB: HOLY SHIT! OK, ok, ok guys, ok. It's ok. I'm ok, you're ok, we're all ok. Ok. Let's just chill. I'm cool. Whatever you guys want to do, that's what we're going to do. I'm going with you guys now, ok...ok. I just have one request.

EMT: What is it, sir?

DB: Please stop calling me sir. My name is Daniel. Please. Just call me Daniel.

EMT: Ok, Daniel. Just relax, we're almost at the hospital...

I woke up with Dan standing at my bedside. Blood was crusting in long smears across my hands. An IV taped to my arm. I had wondered how it felt to have an IV, and now I could see that it felt like very little. I grabbed Dan's hand.

DB: *Dan!* What the fuck is going on, man? Am I in some sort of medical harm? Where are we? Do we need to get out of here? I trust you. You're the only one I trust. If you say rip this IV out of my arm and make a break for it, I'll do it.

Dan: Dan. You're ok. You fell down and hit your head. You're in the hospital. The doctor is going to stitch you up and then we're going to take you home.

DB: Ok, Dan. I trust you.

Dan: Just lay down. Relax. It's all good. DB: Dan! What the fuck! Where am I? What are these tubes? Am I in danger? What are we doing here? Dan!

Dan: Dan, don't worry, man. We're in the hospital. You fell and hit your head and they're going to stitch you up. Just chill.

DB: Ok, Dan. You're the only one I trust. You just tell me what to do. Ok, Dan?

Dan: Ok, then just lay down.

Dan told me later that we had that conversation over and over for twenty minutes. I do remember that the lights were on like I was a Martian dissection, strapped to a board, head in a plastic cone. The Doctor burst in with a flash of his long white coat.

Dr Fischer: Hello, Victor. We're going to get you all cleaned, stitched and sent home with your good buddies here.

DB: Call me Daniel.

Dr Fischer: Ok, Daniel. I'm Doctor Fischer.

DB: Fischer? Shit.

Dr Fischer: What's… the problem?

Dan: His ex. Her last name was Fisher. Since she left, he's been… like this, I guess.

Dr F: Is this going to be an issue?

Dan: No, of course not. Dan. Please relax. Can you relax?

DB: Let's do it.

Dr Fischer: Ok, Daniel. Your ticket out of here is simple. All you have to do is remember three simple words. Once you can repeat these three words back to me, you will be free to go.

DB: Ok.

Dr Fischer: Mountain, tree, cow. Mountain. Tree. Cow. Can you repeat those words back to me now?

What kind of idiot can't remember three simple words? Even as he had said them I was using mnemonic devices to record them. There was a… sunset… and a… cloudy sky… some kind of… animal, yes there was an animal, a majestic animal with horns, maybe a deer. Yes. A big, beautiful deer!

DB: Volcano, sunset… something. Damn I just need the last one! What's the last one? Dan?

Dr Fischer: Don't give him the answer.

I looked over at JF's hallucinating eyes. *I'm sorry,* I said, telepathically.

Dr Fischer: It's important that he stays under our supervision until he's able to think clearly. He waltzed out.

DB: Dudes! What are the words?

My friends obediently let me remember for myself.

A male nurse sprayed cold water into the hole in my forehead to clean out sidewalk pebbles. I asked him what was next. He said, "Well, we just stitch you up and send you home."

I said, "no, I mean, what's *next*. As in what's the next level of depth below the current hole in my forehead."

He said, "Oh. Bone. The next level down is your skull."

Dr Fischer strode in and stitched my forehead with a few quick flicks of his wrist. He tested me. Again, I visualized a misty sunset over a volcano and, in the foreground, a deer. An hour and half later, clarity. Finally.

DB: *Fischer!* I've got it. Mountain. Tree. COW!

I was free.

LAO LAO

Vientiane, Laos

A twelve hour bus ride is a good time for whisky.

He wanted whisky,
I wanted whisky.
Our girlfriends were along for the ride.

We were stopped in Laos, at a bus stop full of dust and dead chickens. Lukewarm meats spun slowly over orange coals while lazy fans with fly swatter arms waved the warm air like slow hands.

Everything is better with hot sauce.

The country is named Laos,
pronounced Lao
and if you say it twice:

Lao Lao,

it refers to clear, homemade moonshine
in used Pepsi bottles.

I stepped off the bus and I wanted this liquid.

There were two passengers haunting this market stall-by-stall.

An Estonian man and his Polish girlfriend.

He wanted whisky for the road,
she wanted peace.
Somehow they didn't know the magic words:

Lao Lao.

I don't know what the fuck he was saying
but the little meat-selling ladies weren't understanding.

I jogged over.
Kindred souls.

Lao Lao!

She nodded and pulled a gasoline bottle from under the table
of old biscuits.
I used my arms to explain that we wanted a full bottle.
I think it was two American dollars.
She overcharged us, I'm sure.
It was mostly rubbing alcohol.

We got back on the bus,
if you'd call it a bus.
A junk yard on wheels
driven by a drug addict
through the night.

They turned off the lights
and we drank to our lives.

RAIN IN EAST TAIWAN

Doulan, Taiwan

JT went to bed with the German girl.
We'd been staring at the rain all day.
I stayed up, sitting outside a 7-11.

A twenty-something Taiwanese guy came up and we talked for a while in broken English.

Amidst other things, and discussing his vocation as a bass guitar builder, he asked me if I'd be interested in sharing a drug that his friends said was like MDMA but that he couldn't be entirely sure of.

I shrugged and said sure before really thinking it through. I'm down for whatever, I said. He smiled wickedly and said, YES!? You sure!?

Let's do it.

I come back 20 minutes! Wait, ok? He slid his maroon hood over his moppy hair and jumped out of his chair, into the rain.

I wrote a note and slipped it under the hostel-room door:

```
JT/T – It's 1am and I'm about to
get into some funny business. I may miss our
9am breakfast. How's that for vague?
```

I hurried across the street, bought a big water bottle and sat to wait for the late night to unfold.

He emerged from the darkness with two little yogurts, a tea candle, an iPad, a portable speaker, and said, *Oh, and paper and pens, yea!*

The little baggie came out as it always does. Chunky brick-colored powder tapped onto our palms. The size of a few big raindrops. As with cliff jumping or anything involving heights, I remember not to hesitate. That bitter pill taste chewed my tongue. Strawberry yogurt drink chaser.

Ambient music. Flickering candle. Talking about things neither of us will remember.

Are you *K'yang!?* He asked.

What's *K'yang?*

K'yang means like, *K'YANG!* He smacked his palm into his temple and rattled his head as if it was spring-loaded. You on drugs! Me on drugs. *K'yang!*

He suddenly seemed a bit more in focus. My eyesight was improving. The little details. The ambient light.

Mmmhmm. I'm a little *K'yang*. You?

Oh yea! I'm *K'yang!* He hit his head again. Back and to the left…

Let's go for a walk, I said. I always say that.

We packed up as our hands began to lose accuracy. We walked into the darkness. Somehow the rain had stopped. *Has the rain really stopped?* A light mist.

Parsing our words into syllables and short phrases came naturally. Speaking slowly, each word a deliberation. Emphasizing. We began to rant about God and death:

The indigenous people
from everywhere Egypt Europe South America Asia
They made pyramids and yet
they didn't know each other existed,
mostly.
No Internet, phone, radio
nothing
and somehow, *somehow*
they built pyramids. As if, somehow,
humans *know* to build pyramids.

Also,
they all created God!
Or, Gods!
They *ALL* believed in something *invisible,*
something greater,
something beyond what they could see.
How is THAT possible!?
I could see MAYBE one or two cultures
believe in God

but NO! They ALL believed.
They all believed in a God or Gods, some force WITHIN
or above
or EVERYWHERE.
Some fundamental piece
inside us BELIEVES!
Knows!
There is something beyond those trees
those stars.
You and me,
we know it!

There are BILLIONS
of people on the earth.
BIIIIIIIILLIONS
Asians and Africans and Americans and Europeans...
and nobody
NOBODY
knows what happens when you die.
We have been to MARS,
and we have NO IDEA what happens.
We have science and technology,
and, yes, we have religion
with heaven and hell
and everything else.
But NOBODY KNOWS.
Not one person.

Yes. There are people that say they've died and come back.
There are people who BELIEVE they know. Who THINK they
know. But nobody,
nobody

ACTUALLY
knows.
Not one person in the six billion
actually knows.
AND
anyone who *says* they know
really just *thinks* they know
and they *know* it's just faith
and they BELIEVE.
But deep down they know that they don't know.
And it's in that not knowing
that we are free.

WE ARE FREE.

It doesn't matter if you are a good person or bad person
or rich person
or crazy person
or poor person.

IT DOESN'T MATTER,

ultimately,
because nobody knows what ultimately matters.
You are FREE.
I am FREE.

We can do anything we want.

In fact, it's the ONLY THING we CAN do.
Anything. ANYTHING. And if anyone says anything... just remember that THEY DON'T KNOW EITHER!

NOBODY KNOWS!

We made our way down to the edge of the wild sea, where waves smash on boulders, and we soaked ourselves in the sounds.

Dan. DAN! We must go. I'm sorry. The sea will come. And high. Too high. Then we dangerous.

Ok.

We walked back through the dark road, through the imaginary forest where the trees became barking dogs and giraffes. We sat back at our table and lit a tea candle. A trio of drunk teenagers smoked cigarettes and hid in a Port-O-John when a cop car patrolled.

After 4am, the *K'yang* gave way to exhaustion. As I stood to go, he handed me a blue marker and asked me to draw something. I drew a symbol on his forearm. He asked me what it meant and I said it means *all good things.*

I hugged him, knowing we'd been to the edge and back and would never see each other again. As I walked to my house, the rain began to drizzle down again.

CAYMAN

Pucallpa, Peru

After four or five hours of intense hallucinations, I found it challenging to walk through even a passable, manicured jungle trail. But this particular night was a full moon and not only did I think I could walk, I thought I could do so with only natural light.

Chris has a pragmatic, zombie-stroll style of ayahuasca strolling while mine is erratic and unpredictable. We crested a berm next to a dark pond.

Now would be an important time to NOT fall over to the left.

We laughed hysterically. Falling into the dark waters of an Amazonian lake at 3am — the clutches, the fangs, the teeth!

Chris flicked on his headlamp. A few steps ahead on our trail glowed two shiny, orange eyes.

Holy shit.

Chris' light illuminated a kayak-sized lizard standing on the berm. There was no way around it. It was staring at us. I think it was making eye contact, but I was on drugs.

I thought of so many things to say: ironic things, things about symbols, funny things to make Chris or the cayman laugh, but I said nothing.

I remembered to breathe into the moment, so I tried that. The clouds were spotting the night sky like leopard skin.

What should we do?

We stared and it stared back. I remembered to connect to the energy of animals, so I tried that. I didn't know how to tell if it was male or female. It was lonely and angry because it was lonely. It thought it was the only one of its kind.

It turned and slid down the berm. It sank under the murky water, turned and looked up at us from a half-submerged head.

We walked as cautiously as we could along the path that the cayman had been standing on, keeping headlamps pointed at it, while trying not to fall sideways. It became increasingly difficult as we became parallel with it, then as it regressed behind us. Would it chase us from behind? I remembered to run zigzag from crocodiles, and was glad that this is my general style of walking. There were a few steps that could have been disastrous for us, but perhaps good for the croc if it wanted to eat us, but I didn't think so.

It just wanted to see what was going on, like we all do.

Ten seconds of stumbling, concentrated silence, then, we screamed: *Holyshitholyshitholyshit!*

We make it holy when we're scared and when we're relieved.

HIGH TEA

Colorado, USA

In The Golden Palace, there's one wrought-iron balustrade that's upside down. The hatted women in the tea lobby sipping under an ornate chandelier from days long past — they don't know or don't care and don't crane their necks to seek out this anomaly.

The champagne comes in little appropriate flutes with three fruits on top, a raspberry, a blueberry, and a blackberry, spiked through with a translucent toothpick. The champagne is mixed with a pink alcoholic twist that some of the women who have sensitivities or have to drive, decline.

A three-tiered platter of nibbles and bites arrives. Scones on bottom, little open face triangular sandwich quarters (cucumber, egg salad) in the middle, and sweets, the waitress points and says "tartlets, and so on", among other words.

An old man plays songs on an old piano that old ladies eating little sandwiches find to be pleasant background music.

The tea arrives in silver teapots.

A woman who's sole duty it may be to pour long ribbons of boiling water from a long-spouted silver urn clasps each silver teapot in order, eldest-seeming or most-prestigious-seeming first; youngest male last. As this woman pours, all eyes transfix on the expertise of her hands and the sudden, amazing danger that this water has brought. All breaths are held. Not an eyeball risks the juvenile game of Eye Spy for this balustrade, even if to pontificate such an affront to the orderliness of things. This intentional removal of each crust, not a gaze is lifted from this game of manners and alcohol and caffeine and sugar — all enlivening and joyful — all obstacles, for your pearls, daaaaahling, become twisted or your broach is askew — the twinkling tune of the crooked old man must not get to you, sweetheart — it must not show: the mortal lust for sweets must be managed; the rush of alcohol into the soft, conversational frontal tissues of the personality must be eagerly brought to bear; and as the caffeine jitters begin to wrack the subtle, polite twirling of the little stirring spoon — fresh Devonshire cream upon the full moon of the gingerbread scone; the sentences are snapping together like channels flipping through, the sandwiches are politely reordered, grinding teeth biting their own lips, some reapply their lipstick in the powder room, and someone glances up as she meanders back to the table; suspicious from under a hat; then an "Oh, do you know the story of that balustrade?" and it ripples from the know-it-alls fired up on their black tea, to the curious, disoriented by second servings of champagne so early in the afternoon; to the prudent, who slam down a few extra chocolates and tartlets without being seen — and soon the ripple is complete, the twelve thirty seating politely excuses itself, one lady at a time unhinges herself from a puffy, high-backed, embroidered chair, slides her gilded wrists through a furry, cuffed, day coat, shoulders her little purse and offers a thin wave before turning towards the door.

A man with a long uniform coat and black leather gloves smiles warmly and bids her adieu; and one-by-one they spiral through the gold-edged revolving doors into the brisk, concrete afternoon.

IV

DEATH

THE BUZZER

Boca Raton, Florida, USA

Nona: DAAAAAN-YAAAAAAAAAAAALL!

DB: Jesus! What?

Nona: Daniel. It's late already. Make yaself a sandwich.

DB: Yes. Right. Ok. I just had lunch actually.

Nona: Wha'd ya have?

DB: Chicken from last night. With Poppi.

Nona: Poppi ate with you?

DB: Yea, we both ate that chicken from last night.

Nona: Daniel. Do me a fayva. Look at my hair.

DB: It looks fine, Nona. You have more hair than I do.

Nona: I used to be beautiful, believe me. Do you think I should shave it?

DB: Like my dad, with a razor?

Nona: No, with that buzza that you use.

DB: It doesn't look bad, but if you want, I'll buzz it for you.

Nona: Would you do that fa' me?

The halo of wispy strands around her head. Aunt Rhonda stood behind us, videoing into the mirror, three of us stacked in the carpeted bathroom.

DB: I always start buzzing right down the middle, that way I can't back out.

She just looked in the mirror.

DB: I'm just saying what I do.

The buzzing of the little machine. I fed pinches of hair into the tiny teeth.

Rhonda: This is not a Facebook picture, definitely not.

Nona: Well, don't put this on Facebook then.

Rhonda: Some people put everything on Facebook. They put their chemo treatments. I don't like that. I mean, I don't mind, I just wouldn't do it.

Nona held her plastic oxygen tube to her nose.

Rhonda: Ma, can you put the oxygen behind ya ears, it'll be more artistic. Right now it looks like ya' holding a mustache.

Finally, Nona said, "That's enough, I can't look at myself anymore."

Nona: My brotha Arthur is going to buy me a wig tomorrow. If you have time, it would be great for Poppi if you could drive us.

The next day, we drove to a wig store in a strip mall in Aventura. Creepy stacks of faceless foam heads with fake hairdos. Art was sitting in one of the two spinning hair-dresser stools. I wheeled Nona up to the big mirror.

Art: How are ya, beautiful?

Nona: Tell the truth I feel like shit.

Art: It's all that chemo, babe. Don't worry, you get ya strength right back. You're in the dip. Afta the dip, it's all gravy.

Nona: Yea? I hope so.

Art: Look. I picked these two for you. One is nice an' short an' easy. The other one's a little longer. Come. Try them on and let's see which you like best.

Nona: I neva had short hair. I just always pulled it back.

Art: You can't put a wig in a ponytail, love.

Nona: I know, I just need to get used to it. I neva had hair like this.

Art: Ya look great, kid.

Nona: You're so full of shit.

Art's wife wheeled Nona next door for what we knew but

could not say was her last manicure and pedicure.

The men ate pizza next door. Art told a long, old-fashioned, joke where the punchline was she had a huge vagina. He was a famous funny man once. He did comedy routines on Johnny Carson before he fell from his window and paralyzed his legs. Now he owns a build-your-own frozen yogurt shop on Boynton Beach. He has the same health issues as Christopher Reeves. As Superman, while Superman was
still alive.

Art shouted text messages at Siri. We met back at the cars. Nona was slumped in the heavy wheelchair we'd stolen from the hospital. Shiny new wig-helmet combed forward. Miss Scarlet fingernails. Her eyes, two pleading black lagoons. She reached up for Arthur. He leaned down on his metal arm-brace crutches and let her hug his neck.

Art: Cawl me in a few days, doll. When ya start feeling beta we'll come and bring some dinna.

Nona, nodded, her face balling up.

Art: Ya look great, kiddo. Really, dahling, you're a knockout. Victa, I always said you never deserved her. Ya just a Syrian prick and she's such a beaut.

Nona waved her tissue at Art, then folded it over her nose. This is how we love each other.

Art: Alright, sweetheart. Drive safe. I love you. Ok. See you soon.

I shook Art's hand and said, "You did a good thing. You made her happy. Thank you." He looked at me and then he turned and clicked away on his crutches. I helped her into the front seat in slow motion. Her matching polished toenails.

Nona: I have such a good brother. How am I so lucky?
I'm so lucky.

She covered her face.

Our black car zig-zagged across the strip mall parking lot as she wept out the window into a fistful of white tissues.

One by one, she was waving good bye to us.

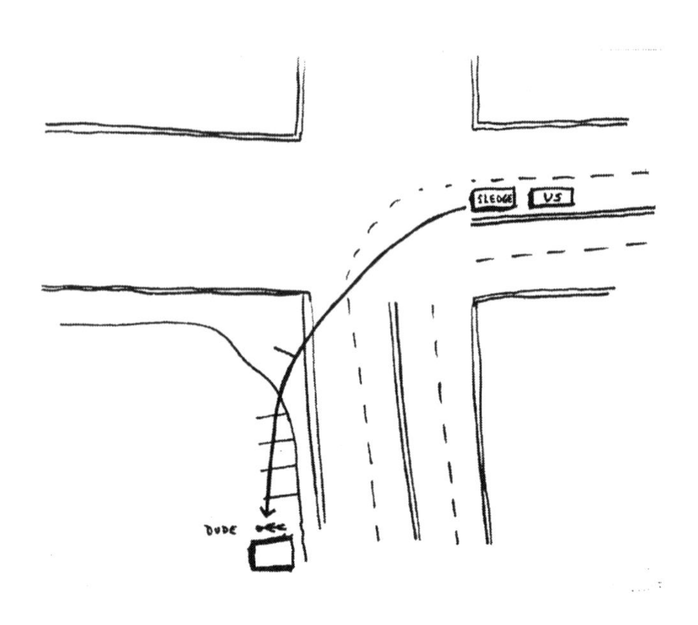
SLEDGE
US
DUDE

SLEDGEHAMMER

Berkeley, California, USA

Mel and I were stopped at a red light, reminiscing about the time I stayed in her parents' house while a poison oak rash ravaged my skin so fiercely we thought it was an STD.

We were in the left turning lane, second in-line behind a beige SUV. It was an Explorer or some rectangular beast with curved edges like the head of a sledgehammer.

Our left blinkers.

The driver of the caucasian-colored sledgehammer waited for the green arrow, then took a graceful, arcing left through the intersection. His tires traced the painted dashes on the pavement. Perfect.

As far as I know, he died immediately thereafter. He died while taking a left. Or had a seizure, heart attack, narcoleptic fit, or in some essential way closed his eyes and left this reality for the next half hour at least.

Unsuspecting Dude was wearing a stupid red polo shirt with the OfficeMax® logo embroidered on his heart when the dead guy's sledge hopped the curb, knocked down a light pole like a spare bowling pin and bounced jerkily into the parking lot.

There was nobody in control. He didn't see it coming.
He stood next to the driver's door of his SUV and dug into his

pocket for his key. The sledgehammer of broken bones was relentless. The grill was an angry face. It pounded his twiggy human body into his SUV, bounced back and stalled.

Unsuspecting Dude crumpled to the pavement.

Imagine that.

The car in front of you makes a left turn, drifts wide, too wide, hops a curb, hits a light post and then — OH GOD NO smashes into a dude, crushing him into another car. What would you do?

I can speak for myself and Mel and say she called 911 while I said *oh fuck oh Jesus what the fuck,* navigated into the absurdly large parking lot and parked next to him. He was laying on his back.

I knelt next to him and in a soothing, yet casual voice, said, "hey man. Just lay here. Don't try to move."

He was awake. "Oh, fuck!" He said. What would you say?

His head leaned up to look at me, but his body remained oddly immobile. Then, his head fell back to the pavement and he looked up at the sky.

I held my hands over his hips. I imagined the bones of his shattered pelvis fusing back together. I imagined white light pouring from my hands, soothing his pain, healing his body.

I tried not to think that there was nothing I could do. I tried not to think he was hopeless or crippled or that there was no light coming from my hands — I just kept trying to be a good, soothing presence for a temporary moment in his life. Mel paced the parking lot, explaining the situation to her phone.

An ambulance roared in, screaming sirens. Paramedics swarmed in and I slid away. I glanced into the sledgehammer. A man was still not awake in the driver's seat. His head tilted back diagonally.

That was it. We left.

REST STOP

Outside of Marfa, Texas, USA

I'm at a rest stop on the side of the 10 freeway weeping. *Will I remember this?* I'm in chilled, inky darkness between El Paso and the rest of the world, where you can run out of gas and the stars are startlingly da-da-da-deep in the heart of Texas.

I'm reviewing the situation from Marfa:

Driving into the sunny afternoon.
Pulled over going 75 in a 70.
Cop tells me to get out of the vehicle.
Standing, shivering. It's cold. I'm fine, I keep thinking. *I'm not cold, I'm Dan.*

I answer his barrage of questions honestly. I tell him my mom was sick and I'm driving to Austin to shake out my mind and see our beautiful country.

He runs my info and says he'll give me a warning.

"But, hey, do you mind if I call the K-9 unit to come sniff the car?"

Ok.

He calls it in.

What if I said no?

“Welp. We’d go ahead and get a court order and then we’d stand here on the side of the highway for a long time. Then the K-9 unit would come anyway.”

Because I’m nervous, I keep telling this guy my life story as if he’s not the one threatening me. We chat like old friends,

“Why are you acting so nervous?”

I get this way sometimes.

He asks about weed in Colorado. I have Colorado plates.

I don’t know, I’m a business man.

He’s analyzing my movements. He’s escalated my case. I’m a case. I tell him about web design as if he’s not the one who is putting my freedom in danger.

The dog arrives in a police SUV. The moment of truth.

Was he following a flow chart in his head? If the suspect seems suspicious, then X, if cotton mouth seems evident, then Y. Aren’t we all?

A blacker German Shepherd than I’ve ever seen sits near the back tire, waits for a signal, then lunges toward the car. It jumps into the open driver window and into the back seat

“The dog will smell if there has ever been marijuana in the car.”

Ever?

The dog jumps out and sits by the back tire.

"Ok, that's it."

For some reason, I shake his gloved hand and say *thanks, it was nice to meet you.*

The end of the flow chart. Some kind of Stockholm Syndrome. I get back to the car shaking. I've been standing in the yellow grass for two hours.

But where was I.

Weeping in the darkness feeling far from home.

The man running for Justice of the Peace in Marfa, Texas also makes delicious tacos in an Airstream taco truck. He calls smoking marijuana *poking smot* and laughs everytime he says it. He advised me to stay in the Marfa camp ground.

> *It'll be late by the time you get to Austin.*
> *And it's dark and there are deer.*

Before I stopped, I reached for my phone to check a message. To break the monotony. A poem by Nash about watching hockey with his wife. I let up on the gas for an absent-minded moment to read.

I looked up and a deer had waltzed in front of my car. I whizzed past it by a foot. I'd have driven right into that deer. I'd be dead?

What I don't realize is that I won't get to do the art project that

I drove to Texas to do; that my grandma would die in five days.

I'd be flown to New York for an orthodox Jewish funeral, and I'd still be there a week later, drinking coffee on the third floor of the Guggenheim. It's an Italian futurism exhibit: Combine and Fall Apart.

(Movement of hands pulled together then spreading)

Time for a manifesto.

I KILLED A RAT

Java, Jakarta, Indonesia

I killed a rat.

He was spazzing out and dying on the floor of my bungalow.

Jo said, "I don't have time to deal with a rat right now."

He was slicing garlic for a dead turkey.

I said "I just need to know if it's been poisoned."

"Probably. Just step on it and chuck it far away."

I thought, that's kind of rude to say to me and rude to do to another living thing especially when it's trying to die somewhere private like the area behind the wooden trunk in my room.

"Ok," I said.

I stood in the cleaning closet for a minute and found a plastic scooper. Maybe I could clock it on the head, scoop it up and wing it with this.

It was my best plan so far, until I saw the half-size metal shovel. The height of a leg. I looked out at the rain.

How would I do it?

I couldn't see myself stomping it out like a camp fire.
The crunching of bones. The blood-spill. Where would
the soul go?

I walked to the old house with the view of the Javanese
mountains, upturned the dayglo-green garbage pail,
and there it was.

Quivering, barely able to comprehend life at the bottom of
this garbage.

I was about to chuck it,
but I knew.

I'd rather be put out of my misery.
Dan, you have to put it out of its misery.

If I had eaten some shitty poison and was sure to die, I'd rather
you just do the equivalent of shoot the horse. I hope my family
never leaves me on life support.

I am not a vegetable.
Just kill me when my body is ready to die,
or let me die.
Kevorkian was right.
There was no point resuscitating the rat.

He was five inches long and brown with a thick fleshy tail,
but he was not going to make it.

I turned the garbage pail over in a dirt patch that will one
day be a garden, dug the shovel blade between its shoulders,
turned my head away and pressed down.

His tiny face turned back 180 to look up at me, and his little arms reached up to pull the weight off his neck.

Some survival response.

I hoped, as I said "I'm sorry," that his eyeballs wouldn't pop out of the sockets.

I could tell I was through. The headless body faced into the earth and quivered like it was looking for something down there.

I scooped the body up gently winged it into a mess of viney trees.

The head I buried in the garden. Not so deep that he won't see the light of day again, when I'm long gone.

V

EPILOGUES

RAIN IN EAST TAIWAN

A few weeks later the Taiwanese guy, (his name when spelled in English is DeeGua), sent me this message:

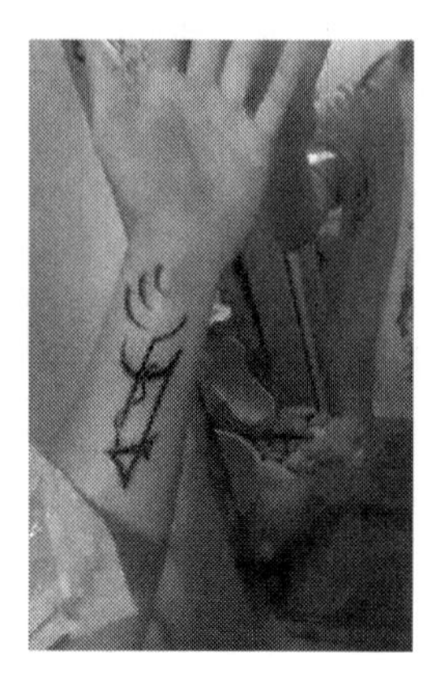

```
I get my first tattoo !!!
to remind me who i am and
what i can do. I made it on
my chinese Lunar Birthday.
All in all ,Danm, I'm sure
people to people have some
connect! :)
U just appear then things
just happen, then I found
myself ;)
It's very very honored to
meet you
```

There was the symbol I had drawn on his forearm at 4am, a message I had encoded while high on drugs, a symbol which means *all good things.*

CAYMAN

Eliza, the shaman who owns the land, said that crocodiles were a symbol of negative energy. But the next day, when I told her that we almost were attacked by the croc, she laughed and said she had to get rid of that cayman — that he'd make a good soup.

ABOUT TURTLES

I want to say "but of course I give a shit about turtles." But I didn't go back and pick up that white bit of trash, and my actions do speak louder than words.

PINE RIDGE

For the record, Richard didn't warn us about not taking photos. I should have know, yes, but I wasn't specifically told not to take photos. I purposely didn't include the photo that got us nearly killed. I am sorry to the Lakota warriors. My intention is to show the strength and power of the Lakota.

THE BUZZER

An email from Poppi:

```
Daniel…Thank you for that e-mail you sent me on
the "BUZZA". It really brought me back. I can't
tell you how much of a help you were to me going
through that horrible experience. It  was almost
like a higher power told you that we were in
need of your help. I'll never forget your "visit
of mercy". I love you Daniel. I can't stop the
tears from running down my cheeks remembering
all of this…Poppi
```

I KILLED A RAT

The next morning I woke up and walked outside my little house. One of the Javanese farmers was planting a juvenile papaya tree directly on the spot that I buried the rat head. They hadn't touched that entire garden for a month. And why he had chosen to plant a papaya tree in the center of the garden, with nothing else… still baffles me. I smiled to him, said salemat pagi (good morning) and walked to breakfast wondering if he had seen the rat head in the garden, and if so, what he had done with it.

SPECIAL THANKS

Mom, Dad, Simone.
Thank you for sharing with me
the extraordinary love of family.

The 3 Dudes,
for making me more than I am.
Master G, Dr K & R-Dog.

My circle of wise friends and confidants
who have crawled with me through much,
and certainly more to come.
Adam, Chanel, Dave G, David H, DeCicco,
Duree, Dy, Eric W, JDP, Martina, Nash, Natasha,
PAL, Peet, Ray, Rus, Tyler, Yang.

The Triforce:
Taylor & Argus.

Rene for believing in these stories
and publishing them in Estonia.

G, for saying "more people should read you."

The Dusty Sneakers for publishing the first story,
A Feast of Morality.

I had a lot of help with this.
I am grateful.

Made in the USA
San Bernardino, CA
07 February 2016